9/00

THE LOUISIANA
PURCHASE IN
AMERICAN HISTORY

Other titles *in American History*

THE LOUISIANA
PURCHASE IN
AMERICAN HISTORY

Ann Graham Gaines

Enslow Publishers, Inc.

40 Industrial Road   PO Box 38
Box 398   Aldershot
Berkeley Heights, NJ 07922 Hants GU12 6BP
USA   UK

http://www.enslow.com

Library of Congress Cataloging-in-Publication Data

Gaines, Ann.
　　The Louisiana Purchase in American history / Ann Graham Gaines.
　　　　p.　cm. — (In American history)
　　Includes bibliographical references and index.
　　Summary: Describes the events leading up to the Louisiana Purchase
and its impact on United States history.
　　ISBN 0-7660-1301-4
　　　　1. Louisiana Purchase—Juvenile literature. 2. United States—History—
1801–1809—Juvenile literature. [1. Louisiana Purchase. 2. United
States—History—1801–1809.] I. Title. II. Series.
　　E333.G26　2000
　　973.4'6—dc21　　　　　　　　　　　　　　　　　99-24659
　　　　　　　　　　　　　　　　　　　　　　　　　　　　CIP

Printed in the United States of America

10 9 8 7 6 5 4 3 2 1

To Our Readers: All Internet addresses in this book were active and appropriate
when we went to press. Any comments or suggestions can be sent by e-mail to
Comments@enslow.com or to the address on the back cover.

Illustration Credits: Alcee Fortier, *A History of Louisiana* (Paris: Manzi,
Joyant & Co., Successors, 1904), pp. 8, 10, 29; Enslow Publishers, Inc.,
pp. 26, 37, 53, 80, 90, 111; Frances Fuller Victor, *The River of the West*
(San Francisco: R. W. Bliss & Company, 1870), p. 60; Independence
National Historical Park, pp. 44, 50; John Bidwell, "The First Emigrant
Train to California," *Century Magazine*, vol. xli, p. 106, p. 58; Library of
Congress, p. 48; National Archives, pp. 93, 100, 101, 108; Reproduced
from the *Dictionary of American Portraits*, Published by Dover
Publications, Inc., in 1967, pp. 12, 14, 17, 63, 73, 81, 84.

Cover Illustration: Independence National Historical Park; John
Bidwell, "The First Emigrant Train to California," *Century Magazine*,
vol. xli, p. 106; Frances Fuller Victor, *The River of the West* (San
Francisco: R. W. Bliss & Company, 1870).

★ CONTENTS ★

R 01718982l5

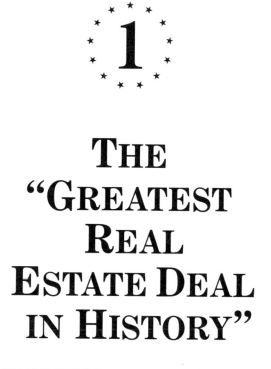

THE "GREATEST REAL ESTATE DEAL IN HISTORY"

On April 30, 1803, United States diplomats Robert Livingston and James Monroe made what has been called the "greatest real estate deal in history."[1] Acting for—but without the approval of—President Thomas Jefferson, Livingston and Monroe completed the Louisiana Purchase. They agreed to pay France $15 million for the colony that the French called *la Louisiane*. When Livingston, Monroe, and François Barbé-Marbois (an official representing the French government) signed a treaty of cession and two documents concerning payment for Louisiana, the United States nearly doubled in size.

The Louisiana Purchase included far more than the present-day state of Louisiana. French Louisiana included the Mississippi River delta and the entire western drainage of the river; in other words, all the lands from which the river and its many tributaries drew water. At the time of the Purchase, no one knew precisely what this drainage basin contained. Explorers

This 1683 French map of the Americas was the first to bear
the name "Louisiana."

had yet to locate the headwaters of the Mississippi and
its tributaries, or the Continental Divide—the imagi-
nary line in the Rocky Mountains that divides
east-flowing rivers from west-flowing rivers.

In fact, the Louisiana Purchase would ultimately
include about 828,000 square miles. Out of this land,
Americans would carve the states of Arkansas,
Missouri, Iowa, Oklahoma, Nebraska, North Dakota,
and South Dakota, as well as most of Louisiana,
Kansas, Minnesota, Colorado, Wyoming, and
Montana.[2] Present-day Spain, Portugal, Italy, France,
Germany, Holland, Belgium, Switzerland, Great
Britain, and Ireland would all fit into the Purchase—
with twenty thousand square miles to spare![3]

France's Acquisition of the Louisiana Territory

In 1803, Napoleon Bonaparte ruled the Republic of France. His official title, in English, was the First Consul of the French Republic. One year later, in 1804, he would declare himself emperor.

When Napoleon decided to sell the Louisiana Territory, it had only belonged to France for a short while. France had acquired Louisiana from Spain by the secret Treaty of San Ildefonso in 1800. Yet France had owned Louisiana once before: on April 9, 1682. After traveling the full course of the Mississippi River and being the first European to do so, Frenchman René-Robert Cavelier, Sieur de La Salle, stood at the river's delta. La Salle claimed all the lands the Mississippi drained for his king, Louis XIV of France. He named this vast country Louisiana.

However, after France was defeated in the Seven Years' War in Europe, it had to give up all its lands in the Americas. In 1763, as dictated by the Treaty of Paris, France ceded all its lands east of the Mississippi to Great Britain. Spain, which already had its own western possessions (including what would become the states of Texas, New Mexico, Arizona, and California), received all of France's land west of the Mississippi.[4] Yet thirty years later, Spain traded the Louisiana Territory to France for, essentially, Tuscany—the rich province containing the famous towns of Florence and Pisa, which is now part of Italy.[5]

Napoleon Dreams of an Empire

During the 1790s Napoleon had hoped to establish a French empire in the Middle East. But his defeat in the Battle of the Nile had shattered those dreams. With his acquisition of Louisiana in 1800, he began to concentrate on building a French empire in the Western Hemisphere.[6] He wanted its center to be what was then called Santo Domingo, the island that now contains Haiti and the Dominican Republic. He expected planters in Louisiana to grow a lot of grain for his Caribbean empire. Louisiana would, thus, serve as a breadbasket.

But his plans went awry. In 1802, Napoleon decided to send his brother-in-law Charles Leclerc to put down a slave rebellion in Santo Domingo. There, Toussaint L'Ouverture, a former slave who had risen to be a statesman and general in the French Army, had taken over the

Napoleon Bonaparte, th leader of France, ha dreams of building a Frenc empire in the Wester Hemisphere. Problems wit his overseas colonies an wars in Europe, however, le him to decide to sell h American holdings.

government. Napoleon foresaw an easy victory in Santo Domingo. After all, he sent a huge, well-trained army to the island. But the former slaves supporting Toussaint L'Ouverture fought fiercely. Moreover, yellow fever raged through the French Army. In the end, twenty-four thousand French soldiers, including Leclerc, died there. The defeat of the French in Santo Domingo dealt a huge blow to France. Napoleon's dreams of an empire in the New World disintegrated.[7]

Thomas Jefferson's Interest in French Actions

In the meantime, United States President Thomas Jefferson observed Napoleon's actions as closely as possible. The signing of the Treaty of San Ildefonso had been a secret affair. Jefferson did not learn until six months after the fact that the huge territory to his country's west belonged to France rather than to Spain. The news shook him; he had long believed that the new United States should, and would, eventually expand across North America and even into South America. He never intended Americans to have to fight to establish such an empire. He just expected Americans to move west naturally. He had not expected the Spanish to offer resistance to American expansion. Spain, once extremely powerful, had become weak. It showed no signs of wanting to take over American territory—or resist American attempts to move west.

As the third president of the United States, Thomas Jefferson supervised the purchase of Louisiana from France.

But the French, he feared, might resist American expansion. Under Napoleon Bonaparte, the military power of France had made great gains. Jefferson also thought it was possible that the British might try to seize Louisiana from the French. Then the United States would be sandwiched between British forces to its north and west *and* its south and west. America's newly won freedom might be in jeopardy.

Jefferson became especially alarmed by matters in Louisiana in October 1802. At the time, Napoleon had yet to establish an actual French presence there. The Spanish were still running the colony. A Spanish colonial administrator issued an order stating that Americans could no longer ship their produce from New Orleans.

Spain had closed the Mississippi once before, in 1784. At that time, Jefferson had worried that settlers of the region, including the Ohio Valley, might go to war with Spain—or separate from United States—in order to gain shipping rights. He wrote: "They [the westerners] are able already to rescue the navigation of the Mississippi out of the hands of the Spanish, and to add New Orleans to their own territory." He went on to speculate that should they do so, "They will be joined by the [French] inhabitants of Louisiana. This will bring on a war between them and Spain, in which the U.S. probably would be drawn on the side of the westerners."[8]

In 1795, Thomas Pinckney, minister to England, had negotiated Pinckney's Treaty. The treaty gave the

United States the formerly Spanish lands east of the Mississippi above the 31st parallel (land that today forms parts of Georgia, Mississippi, and Alabama). Pinckney's Treaty also guaranteed American citizens the right for three years to export "their merchandise and effects" from New Orleans or be granted the same rights at another port on the Mississippi.[9] But in October 1802, the Spanish intendant—the colonial administrator in charge of the district—in New Orleans posted a notice declaring the depot for American goods closed.

This ban represented a huge threat to the livelihood of Americans living along the eastern banks of the Mississippi. Americans who were living in the states of Kentucky, Tennessee, and Ohio, and in the territories of Mississippi and Indiana, profited nearly $3 million every year from goods they floated down the river to

Robert Livingston was t American minister to Fran who negotiated and sign the treaty that transferr Louisiana from France the United States in 1803

New Orleans.[10] So Jefferson asked Robert Livingston, his new minister to France, to negotiate a treaty with the French government that would guarantee Americans the right to use the Mississippi. In March 1803, Livingston received a message informing him that Congress had authorized him to buy the port of New Orleans and that James Monroe was on his way to France to help him negotiate.[11]

Napoleon Decides to Sell Louisiana

On April 10, 1803, Napoleon had a conference with two of his most trusted advisors, Denis Decrès and François de Barbé-Marbois, to decide what to do with Louisiana.[12] He had decided that he could not expand the French colony of Louisiana. In order to get there, French ships would be forced to sail through British-held waters. Although Great Britain was officially at peace with France, Napoleon thought that it would be too risky. There were still tensions between the countries; each distrusted the other and was prepared to take military action if necessary.

Napoleon also had other reasons to abandon his plans for his Caribbean empire, including the colonization of Louisiana. He had begun to think of attacking British-held Malta, an island south of Italy in the central Mediterranean Sea. (Today, Malta is an independent republic.) The next morning, Barbé-Marbois informed him that England was preparing for war with France. Faced with this information, Napoleon suddenly decided to try to sell Louisiana to the United States. Years later, Barbé-Marbois remembered Napoleon declaring, "I renounce Louisiana."[13] Thus he hoped to prevent the United States from turning against France and becoming England's ally in the upcoming war. And the territory's sale would put money that he sorely needed in his treasury. He wanted the offer made to Livingston immediately.

Livingston Meets with Talleyrand

On that same morning of April 11, 1803, French Foreign Affairs Minister Charles Talleyrand sent Livingston a message asking him to come see him at his office. Livingston, prepared to discuss his country's proposal to buy New Orleans, was flabbergasted when Talleyrand opened their conversation by casually asking if the United States would be interested in buying the entire Louisiana Territory.[14] Livingston later wrote:

> [Talleyrand] said, that if they gave New Orleans the rest would be of little value; and that he would wish to know "what we would give for the whole." I told him it was a subject I had not thought of; but that I supposed we should not object to twenty million francs, provided our citizens were paid [what the French government owed them for damages from the French and Indian War of 1754 to 1763]. He told me that this was too low an offer; and that he would be glad if I would reflect upon it, and tell him tomorrow. . . .[15]

That night, Livingston wrote to President Jefferson about Talleyrand's fantastic offer.

James Monroe was sent by President Jefferson to help Robert Livingston negotiate with the French in the hope of buying the port of New Orleans for the United States.

The very next morning, Monroe arrived in Paris. That night at dinner, Livingston met Barbé-Marbois, who informed him that he would be representing Napoleon in negotiations concerning Louisiana. Over the next few days, Livingston and Monroe met several times with Barbé-Marbois. Obviously, they had no way to consult with Jefferson or other American government officials quickly about what they should do. In those days before people could use the telephone or telegraph to communicate between the continents, it took weeks for a letter to go by ship from France to the United States. Monroe had been authorized by Jefferson to offer Bonaparte 50 million French francs ($9.375 million) for East and West Florida and New Orleans. Monroe, Livingston, and Barbé-Marbois bandied about figures. Then suddenly, on April 29, the three men reached an agreement. The United States treasury would pay France 60 million francs ($11.25 million) for Louisiana. It would also pay any claims Americans made against the French for damages the colonists had suffered during the French and Indian War, up to 20 million francs ($3.75 million).[16] In other words, for $15 million, the United States would acquire territory that would double its size.

The following day, Livingston, Monroe, and Barbé-Marbois signed the Louisiana Purchase Treaty between the United States and the French Republic. On May 22, Napoleon ratified it, acting for France. In the meantime, Livingston and Monroe had written home, explaining what they had done. On July 3, Thomas

SOURCE DOCUMENT

ARTICLE I

. . . THE FIRST CONSUL OF THE FRENCH REPUBLIC DESIRING TO GIVE TO THE UNITED STATES A STRONG PROOF OF HIS FRIENDSHIP, DOTH HEREBY CEDE TO THE SAID UNITED STATES, IN THE NAME OF THE FRENCH REPUBLIC, FOREVER AND IN FULL SOVEREIGNTY, THE SAID TERRITORY [LOUISIANA], WITH ALL ITS RIGHTS AND APPURTENANCES, AS FULLY AND IN THE SAME MANNER AS THEY HAVE BEEN ACQUIRED BY THE FRENCH REPUBLIC. . . .[17]

The treaty ceding Louisiana to the Americans was signed on April 30, 1803.

Jefferson received the news that they had completed the purchase. He had some worries that the treaty was unconstitutional, because it had been made without the approval of Congress. However, he decided to submit the treaty to Congress for ratification. The purchase was ratified in the Senate by a vote of 24 to 7 on October 20, 1803.

The American public, upon hearing the news of the Purchase, had mixed reactions. Jefferson was a member of the Democratic-Republican political party, which was opposed by the Federalist party. Many Federalists thought the new nation could not afford the price. A Boston journalist complained, "We are to give money of which we have too little for land of which we already have too much." He questioned why the United States would want "[a] great waste, a wilderness, unpeopled with any beings except wolves and wandering Indians."[18] But others applauded Livingston, Monroe, and Jefferson for the Purchase. On July 18, 1803, General Horatio Gates wrote to Jefferson, "Let the Land rejoice, for you have bought Louisiana for a song."[19]

Spain officially transferred Louisiana to France on November 30, 1803. On December 20, 1803, ceremonies transferring Louisiana from France to the United States took place in New Orleans. A crowd cheered as the American flag, bearing fifteen stars and stripes, was run up the flagpole outside the Cabildo, the main government building. On March 9, 1804, a similar ceremony took place in St. Louis. Louisiana officially belonged to the United States.

LOUISIANA UNDER FOREIGN FLAGS

In 1493, Christopher Columbus returned to Spain and reported on his discovery of new lands. Word quickly spread across Europe. All the great European powers wanted to claim some of the New World. Queen Isabella sent Columbus on a return trip to explore further. In 1497, the English king, Henry VII, sent Italian navigator John Cabot out across the Atlantic. There, he claimed for Henry VII Nova Scotia, Newfoundland, and the Grand Banks—the shoals off Newfoundland where great schools of fish live. In 1500, Portugal claimed Brazil. By this time, French seafarers had also visited the New World, although their king had yet to sponsor an expedition. At that time, the Catholic Church dictated that the faithful eat fish 153 days a year. So French fishermen heavily fished the Grand Banks within ten years of Columbus's first landfall.[1] In 1506, Jean Denys sailed the northern Atlantic Coast. In 1508, a seaman, probably Thomas Aubert, brought American Indians to Rouen, France.[2] In 1513, Vasco Nuñez de Balboa, a

Spaniard, became the first European to see the Pacific Ocean in the New World. In 1519, Portuguese Ferdinand Magellan, commanding a fleet of five Spanish ships, sailed around South America's Cape Horn and then across the Pacific. He died in the Philippines, fighting locals; but one of his ships, carrying just fifteen men, did eventually limp back into a Spanish port in 1522. For the first time ever, humans had sailed around the globe.[3]

In 1524, the French officially became part of the exploring game when King Francis I sent Italian Giovanni da Verrazano to search for a waterway through the North American continent to Asia. (The English would call such a waterway the Northwest Passage.) Verrazano explored the North American coast from South Carolina to Newfoundland. He reported, for the first time, that the North American coastline ran unbroken except by bays from Florida to Nova Scotia.[4] Francis I, unfortunately, was unable immediately to pursue his dreams of an empire in the New World because in 1525, the Spanish forced him off his throne by taking him captive.[5]

New France

In 1527, Francis I came back into power in France and fixed his sights once more on the New World. Pope Alexander VI had declared that Spain and Portugal would divide all lands in the Western Hemisphere. But in 1533, Francis I convinced Pope Clement VII that these two superpowers could claim only lands they already knew. So other crowns could claim any new lands their subjects "discovered."

To take advantage of this decree, Francis I sponsored French explorer Jacques Cartier in three voyages across the Atlantic between 1534 and 1542. Hoping to discover either gold and silver or the fabled Northwest Passage, Cartier headed to the far northern lands in which Spain and Portugal held no interest. He traveled up the mighty St. Lawrence River as far as present-day Montreal, but still found no easy water route to China.[6]

France made its first attempt to establish a colony in the New World in 1541. Seven hundred soldiers and sailors and a few women built a fortified settlement under Cartier's direction on the site of present-day Québec.[7] They abandoned the fort just two years later, however, after they suffered many deaths from attacks by American Indians and scurvy, a disease caused by a lack of vitamin C.[8]

Two more French attempts at colonizing, in South Carolina in 1562 and Florida in 1564, also failed.[9] Frenchmen fished the Great Banks, however, throughout the sixteenth century. These fishermen also started to trade with American Indians for beaver pelts. Between 1598 and 1604, the French Crown sponsored the establishment of a series of fur-trading outposts in Acadia, as Nova Scotia was then called.[10] In 1608, Samuel de Champlain founded Québec. He spent the first winter there with twenty-eight men, twenty of whom died. By 1650, 675 French lived in New

France, in what is now Canada.[11] From 1663 to 1672, the French government actively worked on building New France into an empire, sending six hundred settlers to the New World every year. Many farmed in the St. Lawrence River valley. But others became trappers, who went in search of furs.

De Soto "Discovers" the Mississippi River

In 1539, Spanish conquistador Hernando de Soto let down anchor in Florida's Tampa Bay. He then led some six hundred soldiers on a search for gold and treasure. He took them on an overland trek lasting months and covering thousands of miles through the present-day states of Florida, Georgia, South Carolina, North Carolina, Alabama, and Mississippi.[12]

On May 8, 1541, de Soto and his army came upon the Mississippi River about thirty miles south of Memphis, Tennessee, or eight hundred miles above its mouth in the Gulf of Mexico.[13] De Soto crossed into modern-day Arkansas and that summer marched into the Ozark Mountains. After wintering near what became Hot Springs, Arkansas, he decided to return east and sent a message to Cuba for reinforcements. He was tired, and half of his men had died, killed mostly by Indians. He had found no great treasures. But de Soto never made it back to Florida. On May 21, 1542, just after his men reached the junction of the Mississippi and the Red rivers, de Soto died of a fever. He was buried in the Mississippi River. His expedition had established not one mission, garrison, town, or trade route.[14] The 311 survivors of the de Soto expedition, under the leadership of Luis de Moscoso, built crude boats and sailed down the Mississippi and across the Gulf of Mexico to Panuco, Mexico. When they arrived there on September 10, 1543, they discovered they had been given up for dead.[15]

To the west, another Spanish conquistador had also entered the Mississippi River basin at about the same time as de Soto. In early 1541, Francisco Vásquez de Coronado met a slave of some Pueblo Indians near present-day Albuquerque, New Mexico. The man, whom he referred to as the Turk, told Coronado tales of Quivira, a fabulous country to the east that was rich in gold. He also said that a great river lay beyond

> in the level country which was two leagues [five and a half miles] wide, in which there were fishes as big as horses and large numbers of very big canoes, with more than twenty rowers on a side, and . . . they carried sails, and . . . their lords sat on the poop under awnings, and on the prow they had a great golden eagle.[16]

Coronado took the Turk and, with thirty men, went off to find Quivira. On May 29, 1541, the party stopped on the Red River, the Mississippi's southernmost tributary, in Texas's Palo Duro Canyon.[17] Coronado and his men thus became the first Europeans to set foot in what would become the Louisiana Territory. And they explored a good deal more of the purchase. Coronado would stop searching for the mythical Quivira only in present-day Kansas,

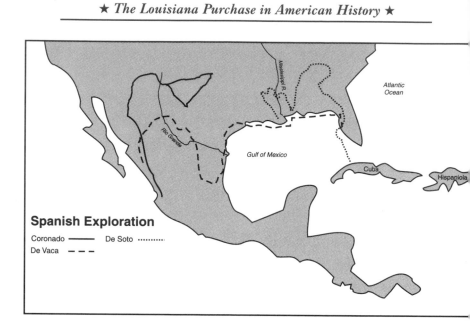

Spanish Exploration
Coronado ——— De Soto ··········
De Vaca — — —

This map shows the routes taken by Spanish explorers across parts of the land that would become the Louisiana Purchase.

when the Turk led him through Caddo Indians' poor villages. Furious at discovering there were, in reality, no cities rich in gold, Coronado had the Turk strangled to death and headed back to New Mexico.

Thanks to de Soto and Coronado, Spain now knew of the largest river on the North American continent and the rivers that drained into it. But the Spanish Crown expressed no further interest in these western lands, which did not seem to be an immediate source of wealth.

Jolliet and Marquette

In the late seventeenth century, however, the French "re-discovered" the Mississippi and realized its potential.

In 1671, French officials declared to seventeen American Indian tribes their sovereign's intent to possess territories from Montreal "as far as the South Sea, covering the utmost extent and range possible."[18] In 1672, French Canadian fur trader Louis Jolliet (sometimes spelled Joliet) and the Jesuit missionary Jacques Marquette, who were searching for Indians to trade with and to convert to Christianity, crossed Wisconsin. They found the upper reaches of the Mississippi River near present-day Prairie du Chien. In 1673, they returned to the Mississippi. Traveling by canoe with five voyageurs, or boatmen, they followed the great river for twelve hundred miles over four months, passing the later site of St. Louis and the mouth of the Ohio River. They turned back where the Arkansas River empties into the Mississippi, afraid of being intercepted by Spaniards.[19]

La Salle

Following Jolliet and Marquette nine years later, Sieur Robert de La Salle canoed down the entire Mississippi River. The French were still extremely interested in the fur trade. The French Crown also continued to dream of establishing a huge commercial empire that would stretch from the St. Lawrence in the north to the Gulf of Mexico in the south. Louis XIV was particularly anxious to prevent Spain and Great Britain from claiming any more land on the North American continent.

La Salle was a Frenchman who had come to Canada to claim a land grant.[20] From Montreal, he went out west, looking to establish trade. In 1678, he sailed through Lake Erie and Lake Huron. By 1680, he had penetrated as far west as the American Indian community known as Kaskaskia, near the present-day site of Peoria, Illinois.[21]

In February 1682, La Salle started his journey down the Mississippi when he entered it at its junction with the Illinois River, north of present-day St. Louis. In the company of about forty Frenchmen and Indians, he passed the point where Jolliet and Marquette had turned back, at the mouth of Arkansas. Ignorant of de Soto's expedition, La Salle thought he was the first European to explore the river beyond the mouth of the Arkansas. Finally, on April 9, 1682, having explored the Mississippi's delta and reached the Gulf of Mexico, La Salle indulged in ceremony. Donning a scarlet coat, silk stockings, and buckled shoes he had brought in a trunk all the way from Montreal, he gathered all his men on the left bank of the river around a pole bearing French King Louis XIV's coat of arms.[22] The Frenchmen prayed and then let loose a volley of musket shots and cries of "Vive Le Roi!" or "Long Live the King!"[23] La Salle then read a proclamation he had written claiming "this country of Louisiana," the entire Mississippi River basin, for his king.[24]

When he returned to France, the French king eventually gave La Salle permission to return to the mouth of the Mississippi on a colonizing expedition, to cement France's claim to Louisiana. La Salle outfitted

Robert Cavalier de La Salle explored Louisiana for France.

another expedition, which sailed in 1684. On this second voyage, however, he failed to sight the mouth of the Mississippi River and unknowingly passed it.

On January 1, 1685, still searching for the Mississippi, his ships reached Matagorda Bay in present-day Texas, instead. This had tragic results. Grounding one ship and wrecking another, the La Salle party was forced to build a fort there. Ultimately, La Salle decided to attempt an overland crossing to Québec. He hoped, finally, to return to Paris to get relief ships to rescue the remaining members of his expedition from Fort St. Louis. To this end, he left there on January 7, 1687. In east Texas, on March 20, having lost faith in La Salle's leadership, one of his own men murdered him.[25] Eventually, six members of the relief party did get to Québec. In April 1689, Spanish Captain Alonso de Léon would stumble across the ruins of Fort St. Louis and later find survivors: two men who would go on to enlist in the Spanish Army and five children who had been adopted by Indians.[26] The rest of La Salle's party had died.

French Colony

In 1698, the French minister of marine and colonies, Jérôme Phélypeaux, the count of Pontchartrain, decided to make a new attempt at establishing a colony in Louisiana. He authorized Pierre Le Moyne, Sieur d'Iberville, to sail four ships carrying 280 men from Brest, France, to the Mississippi.[27] In February 1699, Iberville landed on Ship Island, at the mouth of the

Mississippi in present-day Louisiana. From there, he and forty of his men used longboats to search for the entrance to the river. After four miserable days of torrential rain, they sighted the headland. Finally, on March 3, they entered the North Pass and placid water. Iberville decided, however, not to establish a permanent settlement on the river because he feared supply ships could not enter its mouth. On foot near the present-day site of New Orleans, he met an American Indian, who led them to the present-day site of Ocean Springs, near Biloxi, Mississippi, on the Gulf Coast. There, Iberville's men built Fort Maurepas.[28]

Iberville returned to France for the additional supplies and settlers he needed to expand his new colony. He left his brother, Jean-Baptiste Le Moyne, Sieur de Bienville, behind in Louisiana. During Iberville's absence, Bienville continued to explore the Mississippi. Pierre Le Sueur, a geologist very interested in mining, sailed with Iberville when he returned to Fort Maurepas.

Le Sueur would make a remarkable journey of his own, going *up* the Mississippi, against the river's current, nearly to its source in Minnesota, where he established Fort L'Huillier among the Sioux Indians. After collecting ocher—a yellow powder used in paints and pigments—and ore from mines there, he returned to Biloxi in April 1701. He had demonstrated that if France established towns on the Mississippi, these towns could be supplied directly from the Gulf of Mexico instead of from the Great Lakes.[29] Others stayed in Le Sueur's fort until 1704, when neighboring Sioux and Fox tribes went to war.[30]

In 1702, Frenchmen founded Mobile, in what is now Alabama. It served as capital of the colony of Louisiana for twenty years. In 1706, Iberville died. His brother Bienville became the new governor of Louisiana. France needed to establish a major port on the Mississippi River to control its commerce. In 1718, Bienville founded New Orleans on a high crescent of land free from the danger of flooding. In 1720, France gave up its claim to the Gulf Coast east of Mobile Bay.[31] In 1722, Bienville moved the colony's capital from Mobile to New Orleans, which was described at the time as "an unimpressive clutter of reed-roofed huts and warehouses."[32]

During this period, the French learned more about what they called the Louisiana Territory. French traders went out onto the southern Great Plains to trade goods to Comanche, Pawnee, and Kansas Indians. Trader Etienne Bourgmond began to explore the Missouri River. By 1744, French fur traders had been as far north as North Dakota and into Colorado. So Frenchmen had explored much of the new colony.

French settlement, however, remained extremely sparse. A report from 1743 revealed the territory had a population of around five thousand. Few French went there by choice. Many of those who did go were paupers desperately seeking to leave behind their life of poverty, criminals, refugees from Germany (which was then engaged in war), and slaves.[33]

France Loses Louisiana to the Spanish

In Europe, France was defeated in the Seven Years' War (1756–1763), called the French and Indian War in America. As a result, France ceded to Great Britain all its lands east of the Mississippi River. On November 3, 1762, under the Treaty of Fontainebleau, King Louis XV of France gave all of Louisiana west of the Mississippi River—including New Orleans—to Spain.

Foundation of St. Louis and the Fur Trade

In 1763, word of the transfer of Louisiana from the French to the Spanish had yet to reach the Mississippi. The French government had just awarded New Orleans merchant Pierre de Laclède Liguest a monopoly on the fur trade in upper Louisiana.[34] Laclède especially wanted to trade with American Indians along the Missouri River. That fall, he and Auguste Chouteau set off up the Mississippi to search for a suitable location for a trading post, which they hoped would "shift the hub of the fur trade from Montreal and Michilimackinac to Upper Louisiana."[35]

The following spring, Chouteau, then just fourteen years of age, led thirty men back to the spot they had selected on a bluff twelve miles south of the Missouri's mouth on the Mississippi. There, he directed them in building St. Louis, now in the state of Missouri. By the end of the summer, thirty French families had arrived to settle the town. By the time Laclède died in 1778, the town boasted two hundred buildings and a population of one thousand.[36] By that time, it had become the capital of the Spanish colony called Upper Louisiana.

Spain Returns Louisiana to the French

In the years that followed, Spain administered Louisiana but did little to develop the new property. At the end of the eighteenth century, the Louisiana Territory remained largely unexplored. However, a great deal of traffic did go up and down the Mississippi River. Spain allowed Americans living east of the Mississippi to ship goods through New Orleans. As of 1789, Spain also encouraged Americans to move to Louisiana.

Spain was making some money from Louisiana, thanks to furs and the Mississippi River trade.

Don Antonio de Ulloa wa. the first Spanish governor o the colony of Louisiana.

Nevertheless, when Napoleon Bonaparte expressed interest in acquiring Louisiana in exchange for Tuscany, a very rich and important region of Italy, Spain leapt at the chance. It would continue to administer Louisiana, however, until the terms of the Treaty of San Ildefonso had been fulfilled—until Tuscany had actually been delivered. Bonaparte's interest in Louisiana would very soon fade, however. The French, then Spanish, and then French-again colony would become part of the United States under the Louisiana Purchase Treaty of 1803.

3

LEWIS AND CLARK

No one knew exactly what President Thomas Jefferson had bought when he completed the Louisiana Purchase in 1803. And neither Spain nor France knew what it had lost. For years, the boundaries of the Purchase would be debated. More than that, the interior of the Purchase remained largely unexplored and unknown.

Alexander Mackenzie had crossed Canada from the Atlantic to the Pacific in 1793, becoming the first man known to make this transcontinental journey. The width of the continent, therefore, was understood. Mapmakers had already made detailed maps of the West Coast of North America, which boasted many American Indian villages and some Spanish settlements. Spaniards had explored most of what would become the American Southwest. Still, on maps of the day, the center of the continent remained largely blank. In 1803, cartographer Nicholas King simply wrote "Conjectural" across the lands west of the Missouri on a map he made. Although he showed the Rockies, he drew them in as a short, single line of peaks.[1] Today's maps of the United States show that the Rockies are

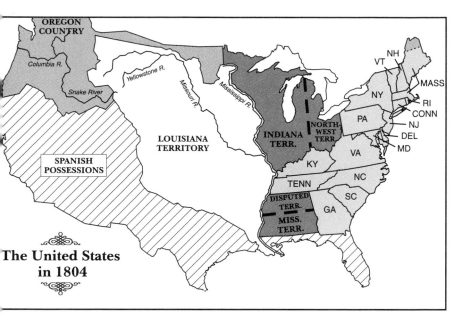

OREGON
COUNTRY

Columbia R.

Yellowstone R.

Snake River

Missouri R.

Mississippi R.

NH
VT
MASS
NY
RI
CONN
PA
NJ
DEL
MD

NORTH
WEST
TERR.

INDIANA
TERR.

LOUISIANA
TERRITORY

VA

KY

TENN

NC

DISPUTED
TERR.

SC

GA

MISS.
TERR.

SPANISH
POSSESSIONS

The United States
in 1804

The addition of the Louisiana Territory to the United States nearly doubled the size of the young nation. But, at the time, the boundaries of the Purchase were unclear.

made up of range after range of mountains that extend for thousands of miles.

Thomas Jefferson probably knew more about the West's geography than almost any other person of his day. His father, Peter, a surveyor and mapmaker, had been interested in the West. Peter Jefferson was a member of the Loyal Land Company, which received a grant of eight hundred thousand acres from the British Crown along the western border of the colony of Virginia. Company member Thomas Walker traveled west to locate lands for company members. He located and named (although he was not the first to see) the Cumberland Gap, which frontiersman Daniel

Boone later passed through.[2] Around 1753, the Loyal Land Company laid plans for another exploring expedition, which never actually happened, this time to the Missouri River.[3]

For years, Thomas Jefferson had been buying books and maps about the West, seeking to learn all that he could. He made especially numerous purchases while minister to France. He bought sixteenth- and seventeenth-century titles relating to Spanish and Portuguese voyages and settlements in the New World. He had copies of the best-known, most up-to-date books at that time about the territory of Louisiana and the Mississippi. He also exchanged letters with many of the most respected scholars and explorers of his age, who told him all they knew about the West. In 1803, Jefferson sent a questionnaire about the West to everyone he knew living on the frontier.[4]

Despite his efforts, the picture of the West he held in his mind was hardly accurate. He thought, for instance:

> that the Blue Ridge Mountains of Virginia might be the highest on the continent; that the mammoth, the giant ground sloth, and other prehistoric creatures would be found along the upper Missouri; that a mountain of pure salt a mile long lay somewhere on the Great Plains; that volcanoes might still be erupting in the Badlands of the upper Missouri; that all the great rivers of the West—the Missouri, Columbia, Colorado, and Rio Grande—rose from a single "height of land."[5]

Thomas Jefferson's Interest in Exploration

Thomas Jefferson earnestly desired to find out all he could about Louisiana and the West. To this end, he started to send out exploring parties even before he became president.

Jefferson had begun to think about the exploration of the continent long before the ink dried on the Louisiana Purchase documents. He himself would never be an explorer. Historian Donald Jackson has called Jefferson "the most towering westerner of them all," but points out that Jefferson himself was no adventurer.[6] He shared his father's love of maps and surveying skills, but never himself felt an overpowering urge to go West. He spent four days, once, on a mule in the mountains of France and Italy.[7] As he neared the end of his presidency, he hoped that he would be able to see the West. In 1809, he wrote, "I have never ceased to wish to descend the Ohio & Missisipi [*sic*] to New Orleans, and when I shall have put my home in order, I shall have the leisure, and so far I have health also, to amuse myself in seeing what I have not yet seen."[8] In reality, he never ventured farther west than Warm Springs, about sixty miles west of Staunton, Virginia.[9] He did, however, possess an unquenchable curiosity about the land.

Jefferson's Earliest Exploring Expeditions

In 1783, for the first time, Jefferson, as a private citizen, became interested in sponsoring an exploring expedition. He wrote to George Rogers Clark, a longtime friend, to ask him to undertake an expedition to the Pacific, saying:

> I find they have subscribed a large sum of money in England for exploring the country from the Missisipi [*sic*] to California. They pretend it is only to promote knolege [*sic*]. I am afraid they have thoughts of colonising into that quarter. Some of us have been talking here in a feeble way of making the attempt to search that country. But I doubt whether we have enough of that kind of spirit to raise the money. How would you like to lead such a party?[10]

Clark had to decline the offer for financial reasons.

In 1785, Thomas Jefferson became the American minister to France. In Paris he met John Ledyard, a Connecticut soldier of fortune who was the first American known to see the Pacific Northwest. Ledyard wrote a book based on his adventures with James Cook on his third voyage. In *A Journal of Captain Cook's Last Voyage to the Pacific Ocean . . . in the Years 1776, 1777, 1778, and 1779,* Ledyard pointed out that a tremendous profit could be made from skins of the otters that lived in the Pacific Northwest. Ledyard hoped to find someone to sponsor him in a trip to establish a fur-trading post there.

Jefferson had become worried that France was trying to add to its possessions on the North American continent when he learned that King Louis XVI had ordered Jean François de Lapérouse to sail across the Pacific to search for the fabled Northwest Passage.[11] Explaining why he wanted to limit European claims to North American lands, Jefferson wrote, "Our confederacy must be viewed as the nest from which all America, North and South is to be peopled."[12]

In an effort to establish the United States' own claim to the Northwest, Jefferson helped Ledyard apply for a passport from Russian Empress Catherine the Great that would allow him to cross Russia bound for North America. Catherine refused the request. She did not want Americans to hunt in Alaska, which was then being heavily exploited by the Russians. Ledyard nevertheless made his way across Russia as far as Siberia. He was headed for the Bering Strait, when Catherine the Great ordered him apprehended and deported.[13]

In 1795, Jefferson solicited subscriptions for an overland expedition to the Pacific, planned by French botanist André Michaux. Acting as a representative of the American Philosophical Society, Jefferson wrote instructions to Michaux in April 1793. He was to accompany a group of Indians from Philadelphia to Kaskaskia, on the American side of the Mississippi. Jefferson also instructed:

> From thence you will cross the Missisipi [*sic*] and pass by land to the nearest part of the Missouri above the Spanish settlements, that you may avoid the risk of being stopped.
>
> You will then pursue such of the largest streams of that river, as shall lead by the shortest way, & the lowest latitudes to the Pacific ocean.[14]

However, Michaux never made the trip. When Edmond Genet, minister from France, arrived in the

United States, he persuaded Michaux to give up his exploration plans. Genet sent Michaux into the Ohio country to talk to American settlers, including George Rogers Clark, about giving up their allegiance to the United States, thus decreasing American power. Genet also hoped Clark would lead an expedition into Spanish territory, thus decreasing Spanish power. These plans did not work out, either.[15]

Jefferson and the Corps of Discovery

In December 1802, Jefferson, ever a determined man and now president of the United States, asked the Spanish king for permission to conduct a scientific expedition into the West. He knew then that explorer Alexander Mackenzie had made the first journey across the continent, in Canada. Writing to officials in Madrid, Spanish diplomat Carlos Martínez de Irujo said:

> The President asked me the other day in a frank and confident tone, if our Court would take it badly, that the Congress decree the formation of a group of travelers, who would form a small caravan and go and explore the course of the Missouri River in which they would nominally have the objective of investigating everything which might contribute to the progress of commerce; but that in reality it would have no other view than the advancement of the geography. . . .[16]

The Spanish refused to issue Jefferson a passport for explorers to use. Nevertheless, a month later, Jefferson asked Congress for money for an exploring expedition. On February 23, 1803, Congress allotted the funds.[17] Jefferson had told Congress that the purpose of this expedition was to establish trade with American Indians who lived beyond the Mississippi. But it was only after the United States had bought Louisiana that Jefferson went full-speed ahead with his plans for what is now called the Lewis and Clark expedition. American explorers then required no foreign country's permission to explore those new lands. They would only be trespassing on foreign land if they passed the boundaries of the Louisiana Territory.

Lewis and Clark

To lead his expedition, Jefferson chose Meriwether Lewis, his personal secretary, whom Jefferson had been training for months in scientific matters. With orders in hand from Jefferson, Lewis went first to Harpers Ferry, Virginia, where he bought supplies such as rifles, pistols, tomahawks, knives, and a folding boat. Then, in Lancaster, Pennsylvania, he took lessons from geographer Andrew Ellicott in determining longitude and latitude. Lewis underwent further scientific training in Philadelphia, where he met Jefferson's colleagues in the American Philosophical Society. He also bought many more supplies in Philadelphia, including fishing lines and "portable [instant] soup."[18] In all, Lewis spent $2,324 getting outfitted.

In June 1803, Lewis wrote to William Clark, a frontier soldier he knew, about assuming co-command of the expedition. In Pittsburgh, where Lewis had had his supplies shipped, he received a positive reply from

Meriwether Lewis was the co-commander of the Lewis and Clark expedition, sent by President Thomas Jefferson to explore the lands of the Louisiana Purchase and beyond to the Pacific Ocean.

Clark. Also there, Lewis hired a boatyard to build a large keelboat for the expedition. This keelboat, or riverboat, could hold ten or more tons of cargo.

What Jefferson ultimately hoped was that Lewis and Clark would find the fabled Northwest Passage across the continent so the United States could establish more direct trade with China. On June 20, 1803, Jefferson wrote a long letter giving Lewis precise instructions regarding the expedition. He informed Lewis that he had already notified representatives of the French, Spanish, and British governments about the expedition.

Jefferson wanted the explorers to make an accurate, detailed map of all they saw. He also asked them to deal very carefully with the Indian tribes encountered. He wanted to know not just their nature, but how many there were and how they were allied. And he requested a report on the soil and face of the country,

SOURCE DOCUMENT

THE OBJECT OF YOUR MISSION IS TO EXPLORE THE MISSOURI RIVER AND SUCH PRINCIPAL STREAMS OF IT, AS BY IT'S [SIC] COURSE AND COMMUNICATION WITH THE WATERS OF THE PACIFIC OCEAN, WHETHER THE COLUMBIA, OREGAN [SIC], COLORADO OR ANY OTHER RIVER MAY OFFER THE MOST DIRECT & PRACTICABLE WATER COMMUNICATION ACROSS THE CONTINENT FOR THE PURPOSES OF COMMERCE.[19]

President Jefferson issued these instructions to Lewis and Clark as they began their expedition through the lands of the Louisiana Purchase.

noting anything—animals, plants, "mineral productions of every kind"—that might aid American settlers.[20] The list went on and on.

In August 1803, Lewis put the keelboat into the Ohio River at Pittsburgh. At Louisville, Kentucky, he met William Clark and nine recruits, with whom he traveled on to St. Louis. There, they discovered that the Spanish commander posted in St. Louis did not know France had sold Louisiana. He had not yet received the news from New Orleans. To avoid confronting the problem of which country now governed St. Louis and the surrounding territory, Clark established Camp Wood on the eastern side of the Mississippi, just below the Missouri, on land that all parties acknowledged was American. His men built huts and started their first map. Clark continued to recruit men to accompany the expedition.

Lewis spent much of the winter in St. Louis, whose residents received a copy of the French and American Louisiana Purchase Treaty in January 1804. He watched Captain Amos Stoddard, newly appointed temporary governor of Upper Louisiana, take possession of St. Louis.[21] There, Lewis also met Auguste Chouteau, who let him pore over his maps and charts of western rivers.

The Expedition Begins

On May 14, 1804, Clark and the "Corps of Discovery," as the members of the expedition called themselves, left Camp Wood.[22] Two days later, Lewis joined them at St. Charles, a French settlement just a few miles up the Missouri. The party appears then to have totaled forty-seven men. Besides the two commanders, there were twenty-seven permanent members, all army men. Another seven soldiers went along to bring the keelboat back down the Missouri later, from the next winter encampment. All the rest were French freelance voyageurs, or watermen, with the exception of York, Clark's slave. Lewis also brought his dog.

For the next seven months, they rowed their fifty-five-foot, twenty-two-oared keelboat and two pirogues—canoes made from hollowed-out trees— against the current of the Missouri, heading north and west. When the current ran too fast or the winds blew hard, they had to get out and trudge along the shore, pulling the heavy boats with ropes. Along the way, they met a few traders. Following Jefferson's instructions, they frequently stopped to talk with American Indians, seeking to build friendships.

The members of the expedition had a few confrontations, including one when they met the Teton Sioux in present-day South Dakota. The Teton threatened to prevent the expedition from going ahead and demanded gifts from the Corps of Discovery. At one point, Clark threatened to fire on the Sioux with a bow gun loaded with sixteen musket balls. In the end, Lewis and Clark had the upper hand in the confrontation, and the corps pushed on.

Along their journey, Lewis and Clark met with Indian tribes, hoping to win their friendship for the United States.

All along the way, corps members kept journals. Lewis and Clark, in particular, carefully noted plants, animals, and minerals that they encountered. They also collected specimens. They named and mapped topographical features and made astronomical observations to calculate their longitude and latitude.

Camping for the Winter

In December, the corps stopped for the winter near present-day Bismark, North Dakota. Snow made further travel too difficult. Their camp, which Lewis and Clark called Fort Mandan, was located just four miles from villages of the Mandan Indians, who had a long history of welcoming Europeans into their territory. One day, veteran fur trader Toussaint Charbonneau arrived at Fort Mandan. Lewis and Clark hired him and his Shoshone wife, Sacagawea, to go along on the rest of the expedition as translators. In the meantime, the corps spent its time hunting, building canoes, and making clothes and moccasins from skins. Lewis and Clark also traded with the Mandan, who told them of the great waterfalls and mountains they would see on the next leg of their journey. Some days, temperatures dipped close to fifty degrees below zero.

In April 1805, the corps set out once again. By now, the French voyageurs had departed. Richard Warfington and six others set off back down the Missouri in the keelboat, carrying scientific specimens and a letter for President Jefferson. Everybody else— the party now numbered thirty-three, including

William Clark, a former frontier soldier, served as co-commander of the Corps of Discovery.

Sacagawea and her new baby—climbed into six new canoes and the pirogues to continue up and around the Missouri's Great Bend. The river narrowed. The land continued to be flat for a time but then became ever more mountainous. On May 24, Lewis seems to have lost his journal when a canoe overturned. From that point on, he and Clark faithfully copied each other's notes, in case of another loss.

At the Great Falls of the Missouri River, in present-day Montana, the expedition had to portage—move boats and supplies overland—for eighteen miles. They attached crude wheels to the pirogues and pulled them overland. The portage was agony. "The prickly pears [cactus] were extremely troublesome to us, sticking our feet through our mockersons [moccasins]," Lewis wrote. Finally, they cleared the falls. Back on the water, they reached the junction of the Marias and the Missouri rivers and had to decide which river was actually the Missouri. There, after much discussion among corps members, they decided to take the south fork. They followed this fork, which turned out to be the real Missouri, until it dwindled away to nothing in the Rockies.

Crossing the Rocky Mountains

Now it came time to cross the mountains. After making their way through Lemhi Pass, the members of the expedition met Snake Indians, related to Sacagawea, who guided them down to the Salmon River and the Bitterroot Valley. Finally, they crossed over the

Bitterroot Mountains of the Rockies through Lolo Pass. Along the way, they suffered terribly from hunger, cold, and sickness. Traveling through snow and hail, even though it was still just September, they became so hungry they killed horses to eat and melted snow to drink.

Beyond Lolo Pass, they were no longer in the Louisiana Purchase, whose western boundary was supposed to be the Continental Divide, the line running through the highest point of the mountains that separates east-flowing from west-flowing rivers. The Clearwater River then took them to the Snake River and the Columbia.

In November 1805, the members of the Lewis and Clark expedition finally saw the Pacific Ocean. On a tall yellow pine tree near the Columbia's mouth, Clark carved in a tree: "William Clark, December 3rd 1805. By Land from the U. States in 1804 and 1805."[23] In doing so, he seems to have been challenging British Canada's claim to the Pacific Coast, where ten years earlier Alexander Mackenzie had painted on a rock "Alexander Mackenzie, from Canada, by land, the twenty-second of July, one thousand seven hundred and ninety-three."[24]

Close to the ocean, Lewis and Clark and their men built Fort Clatsop—really just several log cabins—to wait for spring. On their return trip, the party split up for further scientific exploration after crossing Lolo Pass. Lewis headed north, eventually reaching the Great Falls via the Sun River, while Clark retraced their steps. On August 12, 1806, they reunited where the Yellowstone and Missouri rivers meet, and made the return voyage together. Widespread acclaim followed their return to St. Louis.

Lewis and Clark: Their Findings

In St. Louis on September 23, 1806, Lewis wrote to President Jefferson. He reported that the expedition had found a route travelers could take across the continent. But he also pointed out it was not easy, requiring a trip through the treacherous Rocky Mountains. The long-sought-after Northwest Passage did not exist.

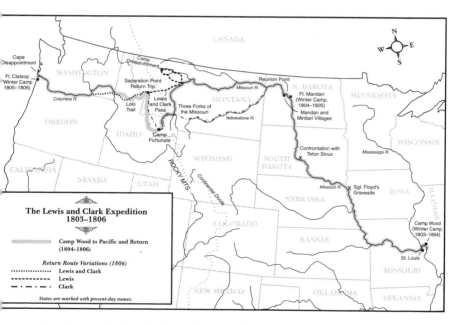

Lewis and Clark blazed a path across the territory of Louisiana to the western coast beyond.

The effect of the Lewis and Clark expedition was profound. It informed President Jefferson and Congress of the wide expanse and topography of the recently purchased lands of the Louisiana Territory and those that lay beyond. But Lewis and Clark's romantic stories of the West's majestic beauty (and its thousands of beaver-filled streams) also did more: They inspired a huge migration of American adventurers to head for the West.

Organization of the Purchase

To best govern the Louisiana Territory, Congress decided to divide the huge region in two. The southern District of Orleans comprised everything south of the 33rd parallel. It contained New Orleans and its many French residents. The northern section became the District of Louisiana. At first, the District of Louisiana, huge in size but with very few settlers, was attached to the Indiana Territory. William Henry Harrison, governor of Indiana, wrote to Jefferson that the population of the District of Louisiana was 9,373, of whom 1,497 were black, the vast majority of whom were probably slaves.[25]

The actual transfer of Louisiana from French to American hands was marked by two transfer ceremonies. The first was held in New Orleans in December 1803 and the second was held in St. Louis in the spring of 1804, just before the start of the Lewis and Clark expedition. Jefferson waited anxiously for word of the New Orleans ceremony. He hoped to hear of it on Christmas Day. But it was mid-January before he learned that the actual transfer had occurred on December 20, 1803.[26] He then appointed William C. C. Claiborne, formerly the governor of Mississippi Territory, governor of the Orleans Territory.[27]

"The first use that Jefferson would see for the new lands west of the Mississippi River, after the Louisiana Purchase of 1803, would be as a vast camp where the Indians could be sent to rehearse the arts of civilization . . . ," historian Donald Jackson has written.[28] To this end, Jefferson did not, at first, encourage Americans to settle there. In 1804, Jefferson himself wrote a pamphlet on Louisiana, which dealt mostly with its geography. That same year, the Sauk and Fox Indians signed a treaty, agreeing to move west of the Mississippi River, becoming the first American Indians to agree to move permanently in that direction.[29]

In 1807, Meriwether Lewis, who had explored the vast new territory for the United States, became governor of Louisiana. He made no great progress toward settling or improving the area, however. He died just two years later, in 1809, while still in office.

THE MOUNTAIN MEN

In the years following the return of Lewis and Clark to St. Louis, many others would explore the new lands acquired for the United States through the Louisiana Purchase. President Jefferson sponsored more expeditions. In 1804, at Jefferson's urging, Congress paid for William Dunbar and George Hunter to follow the Red River to the Ouachita River and then the Ouachita to its source. Two years later, Jefferson persuaded Congress to pay for another expedition in the same region. This time, surveyor Thomas Freeman and botanist Peter Custis, accompanied by twenty-one soldiers, traveled the Red River up past its junction with the Ouachita. They eventually traveled 635 miles up the river, farther than any Americans had gone before. In 1806, too, Jefferson sent Zebulon Pike to explore the western plains.

Yet not all exploration was conducted by the government. Individuals known as mountain men discovered some of the greatest wonders of the Louisiana Purchase.

Frederick Remington drew this sketch of mountain men, which appeared in Century Magazine.

Mountain Men

The traders and trappers who became known as mountain men left a relatively "civilized" life in the United States to fend for themselves in the Rocky Mountains. There, they trapped beaver for their skins, which hatters then used in great numbers to make fashionable men's hats. In the wilds of the Rockies, mountain men hunted almost all their own food. Some married American Indian women, who made their clothes. Others simply made their own clothing. Far beyond settlements with doctors, they also tended to their own health, setting their own broken bones, cauterizing their own wounds—essentially burning away infection—and treating assorted illnesses with herbal remedies they learned from American Indians.

For months upon months, mountain men spent their time alone or in the company of just one or two other trappers or traders. Once a year, however, they would leave the mountains to sell the furs they had traded for or trapped. After 1825, all the mountain men held an annual meeting in the summer where they sold furs and bought necessities such as coffee and sugar. The first rendezvous was held on the Green River. In the years following, the location sometimes changed, but the meeting was always held in the mountains.

Mountain men ranged all over the American West, including the far north and west of the Louisiana Purchase until around 1850. In the 1840s, silk hats became fashionable, and the demand for beaver furs

THE SUMMER RENDEZVOUS.

Mountain men met each summer to trade goods and stories.

decreased. Only this change in fashion trends saved the animal from extinction.[1]

While trapping, many of these mountain men made important geographic discoveries. On the one hand, they explored because it was part of the job of trapping. On the other hand, they clearly considered their explorations important. News of mountain men's discoveries would trickle back to civilization. At first, word of mouth would carry the news—one mountain man would meet another and tell him what he had seen. The second would tell a third, until someone eventually told the story in St. Louis, for example, after which the news might appear in a newspaper or book. A few mountain men made maps that showed where they had been. Others simply told stories about their travels that were repeated. After returning from the expedition he made to the Pacific with the Corps of Discovery, William Clark worked for years on a map of the American West, interviewing traders and mountain men to gain further information.

John Colter

One of the first mountain men was John Colter. A hunter in Lewis and Clark's Corps of Discovery, Colter embraced his new profession even before the expedition formally ended in 1806. He did not return to St. Louis with his compatriots. Instead, he got permission from the co-captains and parted company with the corps while it was still on its return trip, far up the Missouri River.

Colter excused himself from the group near the Mandan Villages because he wanted to join William Dixon and Forest Hancock, traders sent by businessman Manuel Lisa to follow Lewis and Clark's path up the Missouri. Colter, Dixon, and Hancock then headed for a season of beaver trapping on the Yellowstone River.

Colter made particularly important discoveries as a mountain man. During his second season working as a trader for Manuel Lisa, in 1807, he left the fort Lisa had just established at the junction of the Yellowstone and the Bighorn rivers. His exact route is unknown, since he left no written account. What is known is that, in the same year, the Crow Indians of the Bighorn Basin showed him the Shoshone River's geysers in the area geographers now call Colter's Hell. On the same trip, he became the first white person ever known to see Jackson Hole, in present-day Wyoming. In 1808, he also became the first to see lands now part of Yellowstone National Park.

Wilson Price Hunt

In 1811, another area of the Louisiana Purchase was explored, the Dakota Badlands. American businessman John Jacob Astor founded the Pacific Fur Company in 1810. He wanted his men to trap fur on the Pacific Northwest Coast near the mouth of the Columbia River. He planned to ship these furs to China. To stake his claim on the Columbia, he sent a ship, the *Tonquin*, around Cape Horn. Its crew built a small cluster of buildings they called Fort Astoria at the mouth of the Columbia.

A second party went overland. In March 1811, Wilson Price Hunt, a clerk without any exploring experience who had signed on with Astor, left St. Louis with Canadian fur trader Donald Mackenzie and sixty men, including botanists John Bradbury and John Nuttall. They ascended the Missouri to the Arikara Indian villages. There, Hunt decided he would not follow Lewis and Clark's route (although Clark had given him a map). Instead, he would look for a shortcut to the Columbia. He and his men bought eighty-two horses from the Arikara and set off across the Dakotas. They crossed the terrible Badlands and struggled through the Bighorn Mountains. They left

John Jacob Astor, owner of the Pacific Fur Company, was an important figure in the early settlement of the West, and for his role in establishing the American fur trade.

American territory when they crossed the Continental Divide at Union Pass. Beyond, they encountered more hardship. In the winter, they struggled overland between the Snake and the Columbia rivers. Members of the party later remembered eating roots, dogs, horses, and beaver paws to prevent starvation on that leg of their journey.

In February 1812, they did reach the mouth of the Columbia, where they joined the *Tonquin* crew at Fort Astoria. On June 1, 1812, President James Madison issued a war message. Ever since the end of the American Revolution, England had continued to interfere in American trade. Now, Madison hoped to end the unwelcome interference by once again defeating the British in warfare. The War of 1812 would actually be fought until 1814. In March 1813, it caused the

Astorians to abandon their fort under threat of the arrival of a British ship.

Robert Stuart

In his trek to Fort Astoria, Wilson Price Hunt had discovered a new overland route across the North American continent.[2] However, it was fellow Astor employee Robert Stuart who made the Astorians' most important geographical discovery. In June 1812, before the surrender of Fort Astoria to the British, Stuart led a party of six east and headed back to New York. Their trip proved so difficult that one man, John Day, went insane along the way.[3]

Nevertheless, the Stuart party made a momentous discovery when, out of Jackson Hole, they headed not north around the Wind River Mountains like Hunt, but west. At the south end of the Wind River Mountains, they found the South Pass of the Rockies. After this easy crossing over the Continental Divide, they followed the Platte River downstream. They arrived in St. Louis on April 30, 1813.

They had essentially followed in reverse what would become the Oregon Trail. South Pass soon became the gateway to the West, through which many thousands of emigrants would travel on their way to Oregon or California. But for the time being, John Jacob Astor kept the knowledge of the easy crossing a secret.[4] South Pass would have to be rediscovered before the Oregon Trail opened for travelers.

William Ashley

For a time, the War of 1812 and Spanish officials' harassment of explorers who entered the Spanish West suspended exploring efforts in the "stony mountains."[5] But in 1822, William Ashley, founder of the Rocky Mountain Fur Company, brought a large number of mountain men back into the West. In February 1822, Ashley placed an advertisement in the St. Louis *Gazette*. It read:

> The subscriber wishes to engage ONE HUNDRED MEN, to ascend the river Missouri to its source, there to be employed for one, two or three years. For particulars enquire of Major Andrew Henry, near the Lead Mines, in the County of Washington, (who will ascend with, and command the party) or to the subscriber at St. Louis.[6]
>
> William H. Ashley

Those who answered his ad included some of the greatest of all mountain men: Jedediah Smith, William Sublette, Hugh Glass, and Jim Bridger.

Ashley's first season trading came to almost nothing. A keelboat sank, sending ten thousand dollars in trade goods to the bottom of the Missouri. In June 1823, Ashley sent about seventy men in keelboats up the Missouri. Arikara Indians attacked them. Some keelboats were able to retreat back downstream, but many trappers were pinned down on a sandy beach across from the Arikara village. In order to escape the rain of arrows, several of Ashley's best men—including Jedediah Smith and Jim Bridger—had to abandon their rifles and other equipment on the beach, run for the river, and swim for their lives.[7]

Nevertheless, trappers and traders roamed all over the central Rockies after 1822, exploring both the eastern mountains that were part of the Louisiana Purchase, and the western mountains, which belonged to the British and Canada. At the same time, mountain men were exploring south, entering Spanish territory, headed for Taos and Santa Fe.

In July 1825, it was Ashley who held the first meeting of mountain men on the Green River in present-day Wyoming. From then on, mountain men gathered once a year. This was, in essence, a huge trade fair where trappers, traders, and thousands of Indians met to buy and sell furs and supplies, swap stories, play ball, race, gamble, and drink.[8] It continued long after Ashley retired from the fur business.

Jedediah Smith

In the 1820s, Jedediah Smith became perhaps the most famous mountain man and one of the most important explorers of North America. As a young man, he moved to St. Louis, looking for adventure. At age twenty-three, he wrote in his journal that he had read Ashley's ad and "called on Gen Ashley to make an engagement to go with him as a hunter."[9] Smith spent that fall and bitter cold winter hunting meat and trapping beaver near the Mussleshell River in present-day central Montana.[10]

After the Arikara attack in June 1823, Smith led a small trapping party across the Dakota Badlands and into the Black Hills. One day near the Powder River, Smith, leading a horse through a brushy creek bottom, bumped into a grizzly. The bear grabbed Smith and bit his head. His party shot and killed the bear, but they feared Smith would die. His ribs were broken and his face terribly torn up. His friend Jim Clyman later wrote:

> I asked the Capt. what was best he said one or 2 [go] for water and if you have a needle and thread git it out and sew up my wounds around my head which was bleeding freely i got a pair of scissors and cut off his hair and then began my first job of d[r]essing wounds upon examination I [found] the bear had taken nearly all of his head in his capuous mouth close to his left eye on one side and clos to his right ear on the other and laid the skull bare to near the crown of the head leaving a white streak whare his teeth passed.[11]

Jedediah Smith kept the scars of this encounter. For the rest of his life, he had just one eyebrow, a squinty eye, and a torn ear.

Smith recovered speedily. By November, his party had crossed the Powder River and the Bighorn Mountains. They spent the winter with Crow Indians in the Wind River valley.[12] In February 1824, Smith and his men tried to leave the valley, but deep snow blocked the only way out they knew—Union Pass at the valley's north end. When they returned to the Crow village, the Indians spread a large buffalo robe on a lodge floor, and using sand piles to represent mountains, showed Smith that there was another route west to the beaver-filled streams of the Teton Mountains. He simply needed to head around the southeastern end of the Wind River Mountains. Despite the continuing snow, Smith followed the Crow's directions and reached the Sweetwater River. The party turned west. A few days later, Smith noticed that the waters under the ice of the streams they encountered flowed west—to the Pacific. They had crossed the Continental Divide. He, too, had found the South Pass. Smith would continue to explore the American West, until his death at the age of thirty-two in 1831, during an ambush by Comanche Indians.

Legacy of the Mountain Men

Jedediah Smith, William Ashley, John Colter, and the many others like them played a major role in the story of the Louisiana Purchase. As rugged explorers and smart businessmen, they found or carved new routes through the western United States. They also paved the way for others to follow them in western trade and settlement.

ESTABLISHING THE BOUNDARIES

For the fifteen years following the Louisiana Purchase, the United States and Spain, and to a lesser extent, the United States and Great Britain argued over the exact boundaries of the Louisiana Purchase.

The treaty between the United States and the French Republic signed in Paris on April 30, 1803, simply stated that the French Republic ceded the Louisiana territory to the United States. Of the boundaries of the territory, it said absolutely nothing besides quoting the Treaty of San Ildefonso, which said that the province of Louisiana acquired by France had "the Same extent that it now has in the hand of Spain, & that it had when France possessed it. . . ."[1]

When Thomas Jefferson made the Louisiana Purchase, he believed that above the Mississippi River delta, the territory was bounded on the east by the Mississippi and to the northeast by the headwaters of the Mississippi. To the northwest, he thought the Purchase ended at the headwaters of the Missouri. To the West, it ended in the Rocky Mountains, at what he referred to as the height of land, which modern geographers call the Continental Divide. He thought that the Red River, the Mississippi's southernmost tributary, should serve as the southwestern border. He was undecided about whether what then constituted Spanish West Florida should really be considered part of the purchase.[2] France had ceded Florida to Spain in 1763 under the Treaty of Paris, which was signed by the European powers at the end of the Seven Years' War. Spain had then traded Florida to England for Cuba, because it had been part of French Louisiana at one point. Spain took back Florida, however, after the American Revolution. Jefferson questioned whether the Louisiana Purchase Treaty meant that the lands the United States received under it should include Florida, because it had originally been part of French Louisiana.

Over the years, however, Jefferson modified some of his views concerning the boundaries after research-ing earlier Spanish and French claims in his extensive libraries. Representatives of Spain rejected some of the American claims, arguing over the boundaries of the Louisiana Purchase for years. At times, the Spanish used military force to ensure that Americans did not enter what they considered their Crown's lands. Sometimes they even tried to prevent Americans from exploring lands ceded to the United States by the Purchase. For example, Spanish soldiers unsuccessfully attempted three times to intercept the Lewis and Clark expedition.

The Red River

Even as Lewis and Clark explored the northern half of the Louisiana Territory and lands to its west, Thomas Jefferson attempted to find out where, exactly, its southwestern boundary lay. In other words, he especially wanted to determine the exact course of the Red River. To this end, he authorized William Dunbar and naturalist George Hunter to make an expedition there. They left St. Catherine's Landing in present-day Louisiana on October 16, 1804. They started up the Red, but hostile Osage Indians impeded their progress, and they left that river at the mouth of the Ouachita. (The Ouachita empties into the Red in central present-day Louisiana.) Then, they ascended the Ouachita to about the site of present-day Monroe, Louisiana. From there, they explored the Ozark Plateau, crossing into Arkansas and portaging to the Hot Springs.

In 1805, in response to a request by Jefferson, Congress allotted five thousand dollars for a second Red River expedition. In 1806, scientists Thomas Freeman and Peter Custis led twenty-four soldiers, commanded by Richard Sparks, close to six hundred fifty miles up the Red, looking for its source. They had one notable achievement. By detouring down creeks and across lakes and swamps, they were able to navigate in boats around the Great Raft—the huge logjam that blocked it.[4] But on July 29, they met Spanish officer Francisco Viana and a detachment of soldiers near the point where the states of Texas, Oklahoma, and Arkansas meet today. He insisted that they turn back.

Historian Donald Jackson has speculated that Freeman and Sparks were relieved when they failed because they were finding it increasingly difficult to row as the Ouachita became more shallow. Soon they would have had to leave the water and acquire horses to carry them farther. They had also given away most of the gifts they had brought, so they may have feared future meetings with Indians.

Zebulon Pike

In the spring of 1805, James Wilkinson became the temporary governor of the Louisiana Territory. Jefferson had instructed him in his most important duties: He must prevent Canadians—who represented Great Britain—from trading west of the Mississippi, keep the residents of settlements below St. Louis from deserting their communities, and prevent Indians from the Territory of Orleans from being transferred to the Territory of Louisiana.[5]

As a private businessman, Wilkinson planned to send a party up the Missouri River to the Yellowstone to find out what the American Indians along the way had to trade.[6] Scholars have been unable to determine if this party ever actually set out. In 1806, Wilkinson sent trader John McClallen to go up the Platte River. In his official capacity, Wilkinson ordered an exploration of the Osage country of Kansas and Oklahoma in 1805 by Lieutenant George Peter and some Indian traders.[7] Peter accurately mapped the Osage, although it was already known.

That summer, Wilkinson also ordered Lieutenant Zebulon Pike to locate the sources of the Mississippi River.[8] Pike did not do so. Due to the onset of winter, he went no farther than Cass Lake in northern Minnesota. But he succeeded in forcing the British traders he found on the river's upper reaches to admit that they were in American territory.[9]

The following summer, in 1806, Wilkinson ordered Pike to lead another expedition. This time, Pike was to locate the source of the Red River. Although there is no definitive proof, historians believe Wilkinson also gave him secret orders to march all the way to Santa Fe, the Spanish stronghold in New Mexico.[10]

On July 15, 1806, Pike and twenty-three men left Belle Fontaine near St. Louis. They headed west

Zebulon Pike was one of the early explorers of the southern boundaries of the Louisiana Purchase.

to the Osage villages, located near the western border of present-day Missouri. (Pike was to return Osage captives there and work to secure peace between the Osage and the Kansas tribes, who had been warring.) Then Pike's party headed for the Pawnee villages on the Republican River in what is now Nebraska. From there, they headed south until Pike sighted the Arkansas River. There, he sent half his party back down the Arkansas with dispatches for Wilkinson, describing the lands he had seen thus far. Pike himself, with the other half of his men, headed west along the Arkansas. Donald Jackson has written, "The burned-out campfires of the Spanish and the chopped turf left by the hooves of their mounts promised to guide them to and even through the first range of mountains."[11] On November 15, 1805, they sighted the Rocky Mountains for the first time.

That winter, they spent weeks exploring the Rockies as far north as the point where the South Platte River rises in northern Colorado. At one point, they attempted to climb what is now called Pike's Peak near present-day Denver, but failed. From the top of Cheyenne Peak, however, they saw before them all of the southern Rockies.[12] Finally, despite its being mid-winter, Pike led thirteen of his men south toward the Sangre de Cristo River in southern Colorado. He had to leave six of his men behind, crippled with gangrene, or decay of injured tissue. Finally, he and his remaining men reached the Rio Grande, which later they all claimed they mistook for the Red. On the Rio Conejos, they built a fort.

On February 26, 1806, Spanish cavalry arrived and arrested Pike and his men, despite their protests. They continued to claim that they had not realized they had entered Spanish territory, that they thought they were still in the Louisiana Purchase. They were marched as prisoners to Santa Fe and on to Chihuahua. Finally, they were allowed to return across Texas to the United States, where Pike filed a lengthy report for Congress covering all he had seen.

At the time it was published, Pike's work contained the most extensive description of northern Mexico then available to Americans. It also greatly affected western development and settlement. In it, Pike characterized the Great Plains as "sandy deserts" like those found in Africa. He wrote: "I saw in my route, in various places, tracts of many leagues where the wind had thrown up the sand in all the fanciful form of the ocean's rolling wave; and on which not a speck of vegetable matter existed."[13] Pike did not, however, consider the presence of a desert on the American border a problem. Instead, he thought it should constitute a frontier to be inhabited only by Indians.[14]

The Burr Conspiracy

In the summer of 1806, Thomas Jefferson ordered Vice President Aaron Burr arrested for treason. James Wilkinson had charged Burr with plotting with the Spanish to convince Americans living in the West to separate from the United States and form their own confederacy. Eventually, Spain hoped to regain the lands of the Louisiana Purchase. Jefferson considered Wilkinson a hero for turning in Burr. Historians now know that Wilkinson had actually been working for the Spanish himself for years. But during his lifetime, he was never charged with conspiracy. Instead, he continued his wheeling and dealing, later seeking to become a major landowner in Texas, which was then part of a Mexican province. He died in 1825 in Mexico City, where he had gone to apply for a huge grant of Texas land.

The Convention of 1818

In 1818, the United States and Great Britain (which still owned the huge territory of Canada) agreed that the northern boundary of the United States in the West would run along the 49th parallel from Lake of the Woods, located partly in present-day Minnesota, to the Rockies. As a result, the United States relinquished its claim to the very northern reaches of the Louisiana Purchase, because some of the new British land was drained by the upper Mississippi.[15] In exchange, the United States gained title to the headwaters of Wisconsin's Red River (as opposed to the Red River of the American Southwest) as well as the right to administer the Oregon Territory with Great Britain. In 1846, what was called the Oregon Question—the debate of who owned the Oregon Territory—was finally settled. Great Britain agreed that the United

States boundary along the 49th parallel would extend beyond the Rockies to the Pacific Ocean.

Stephen Long

In 1819, British fur traders so regularly trespassed onto American soil that army General Henry Rice Atkinson commanded five steamboats up the Missouri to drive them out.[16] Conflicts with Indians forced all the boats to turn back except for one carrying a party led by Captain Stephen H. Long. Long had accompanied Atkinson in a sixth steamboat, as part of a company of scientists and engineers. After Atkinson's failure, Long and his men continued to explore and map the Great Plains of Oklahoma, Kansas, and eastern Colorado. He carefully directed the mapping of the entire region and then headed into the Rockies. Long climbed Pike's Peak, which Pike had failed to do himself in 1807. Artist Samuel Seymour, who accompanied him, painstakingly made the first drawings ever of the Front Range of the Rockies.

Then Long divided his party. He sent one group down the Arkansas. Members of this party deserted, taking with them Long's maps and notes. Long, like earlier explorers, headed off to look for the source of the Red. He satisfied himself, finally, that he had located the springs from which it rises. Unfortunately, after cruising down the river, he discovered that he had been on the Canadian River instead of the Red.[17] So his explorations did not help solve the problem of where exactly lay the boundaries of the Louisiana Purchase, as he had hoped.

In his final report to the government, Long echoed Pike's earlier assessment of the Plains. On his widely circulated map, Long labeled them a "Great Desert." Settlers took his words so seriously that the area remained largely vacant for years.

The Transcontinental Boundary Treaty

In 1819, the question of the United States' southern and western boundary was finally settled when Secretary of State John Quincy Adams negotiated the Transcontinental Boundary Treaty with Spain. In 1818, General Andrew Jackson had invaded Spain's East Florida, claiming he wanted to stop Florida's Seminole Indians from making raids on American settlements farther north. Because of this military occupation, Spain finally gave in to American demands that the boundary be settled and signed the Transcontinental Boundary, or Adams-Onís, Treaty. In exchange, Spain received trading rights in Florida. The American government also agreed to pay some debts the Spanish Crown owed citizens of the United States. The United States stated that it staked no claim to Texas. For its part, the United States had its southwestern limit settled. The countries agreed that the Sabine, Red, and Arkansas rivers separated American and Spanish territory, and Spain recognized the American claim to the Oregon Country.[18]

SOURCE DOCUMENT

ARTICLE II

HIS CATHOLIC MAJESTY CEDES TO THE UNITED STATES, IN FULL PROPERTY AND SOVEREIGNTY, ALL THE TERRITORIES WHICH BELONG TO HIM, SITUATED TO THE EASTWARD OF THE MISSISSIPPI, KNOWN BY THE NAME OF EAST AND WEST FLORIDA. THE ADJACENT ISLANDS DEPENDENT ON SAID PROVINCES, ALL PUBLIC LOTS AND SQUARES, VACANT LANDS, PUBLIC EDIFICES, FORTIFICATIONS, BARRACKS, AND OTHER BUILDINGS, WHICH ARE NOT PRIVATE PROPERTY, ARCHIVES AND DOCUMENTS WHICH RELATE DIRECTLY TO THE PROPERTY AND SOVEREIGNTY OF THE SAID PROVINCES, ARE INCLUDED IN THIS ARTICLE.[19]

The Adams-Onis, or Transcontinental Boundary, Treaty settled conflicts with Spain over the southern and eastern boundaries of the Louisiana Purchase.

Captain Benjamin Bonneville

In 1832, Captain Benjamin Bonneville became the next explorer working for the federal government to cross the Louisiana Purchase. In May, he left Kansas City and headed west at the head of a caravan of wagons. Slowly, they headed west along the Platte River to the Rockies. His only notable achievement in the Louisiana Territory came when he took his caravan through South Pass, becoming the first to take wagons through it and thus proving that emigrants could do so, too.

In the next year, Bonneville struck out beyond the Louisiana Purchase. By November 1833, his party had

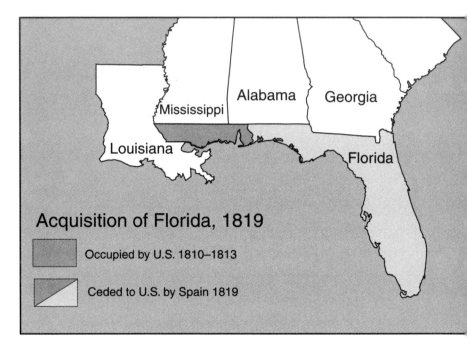

Acquisition of Florida, 1819

Occupied by U.S. 1810–1813

Ceded to U.S. by Spain 1819

The Adams-Onis, or Transcontinental Boundary, Treaty ceded parts of Spanish Florida to the United States.

reached California. Under Bonneville's direction, Joseph Walker found a practical emigrant trail to California the following year.[20]

Frémont, the Pathfinder

In 1842, Senator Thomas Hart Benton persuaded Congress to sponsor his son-in-law, Lieutenant John C. Frémont, in an exploring expedition into the Rockies. That summer, after crossing through Missouri, Kansas, Nebraska, and Wyoming, Frémont led his men to the headwaters of the Sweetwater River and beyond, through the Wind River Mountains and South Pass.

In 1843, Frémont was sent on another—this time secret—mission by Benton. Guided by old mountain men Kit Carson and Joseph Walker, among others, he and his expedition circumnavigated the West. They marched across the Louisiana Purchase and into Oregon and California. Then they returned through the southwestern desert.

John C. Frémont became known as the Pathfinder, for his journeys through the Louisiana Territory.

Because of these exploits, Frémont became known as the Pathfinder.

In 1845, Frémont conducted another unofficial expedition to the West. With a tough crew of seasoned mountain men, he marched back to California, which was still owned by Mexico. In June 1846, Frémont and other Americans seized the town of Sonoma, California, and established what they called the Bear Flag Republic—an independent nation. Americans soon controlled California, although Mexico did not formally cede it to the United States until after its defeat in the Mexican War in 1847. The gold rush that began in California in 1848 triggered a tremendous emigration to California, much of it overland through the Louisiana Purchase.

Throughout the United States' history, seemingly every American has had a vivid image of the West in his or her mind. Today, we get that image largely from Western films that always seem to feature lawmen, cowboys, and Indians set either in a dusty, one-street town or out on the lone prairie.

THE IDEA OF EXPANSION

Americans' Vision of the West

But the American fascination with the West is hardly new. In the seventeenth century, American colonists already saw the frontier—which was what is now the eastern portion of the United States—as a place of adventure and danger. One resident of a seaboard town in Massachusetts recorded in his diary that he had seen his daughter off on a trip of fifteen miles. She was going to visit relatives in a settlement farther inland, and he wrote, "I did greatly fear for Abigail's safety, as she is gone into Duxbury. It is her first journey into the West, and I shall pray mightily for her early return."[1]

Settlement

By 1713, most American colonists still lived within fifty miles of the Atlantic Ocean, but settlers were about to expand the frontier. By 1750, one third of the population had moved to the Piedmont of the Carolinas.[2]

Historians often refer to Daniel Boone as the first westerner. Born in Pennsylvania, he fought in the French and Indian War. Then he started roaming, first in Florida and then to the West. He lived for a time in the Great Smoky Mountains.

Over and over, he searched for an easy trail into what is now Kentucky. While doing so, he was captured and adopted by an Indian tribe from which he eventually felt the need to escape. He nearly died in a blizzard, and once he almost drowned. In 1775, he and thirty fellow woodsmen cleared what would be called the Wilderness Road from eastern Tennessee

Daniel Boone is sometime called the first westerner.

through the Cumberland Gap to the future site of Louisville, Kentucky, on the Ohio River. When news spread about this feat, Boone became the subject of ballads and tall tales. Inspired, more than one hundred thousand people moved into western Tennessee and Kentucky in fifteen years.[3]

During this period, many settlers suffered raids by Indian war parties on their isolated frontier settlements. Between 1784 and 1790, more than fifteen hundred settlers of Kentucky were killed or captured by Indians, who resisted white settlement on their tribal lands. By this point, white settlers seem to have cemented their attitudes toward the displacement of American Indians. They believed it was their right to stay in Indian territory. Writing about how settlers had begun to retaliate in answer to Indian raids, an army officer wrote, "The people of Kentucky will carry on private expeditions against the Indians and kill them whenever they meet them, and I do not believe there is a jury in all Kentucky [that] will punish a man for it."[4]

Expansionism as an Idea

The West did not preoccupy much of George Washington's time when he served as the first president of the United States. As a young man, he had seen and owned land in the Ohio Country, which was then far in the West. But the business of organizing the new United States government fully occupied his time. Later presidents, however, spent a great deal of time considering how the West should be used.

At first, Thomas Jefferson did not think the United States should create new states in the Louisiana Territory, the new lands between the Mississippi and the Rockies.[5] Then, public consensus grew, and Jefferson came to accept the idea, with which later presidents also agreed. The sixth president, John Quincy Adams, was the first to say that he felt the United States should extend from sea to shining sea.

In the years that followed, expansionists adapted ideas from Thomas Jefferson, John Quincy Adams, and other early United States leaders who believed that Americans' westward movement would continue until they reached the Pacific. In 1844, James K. Polk was elected president. His opponent, Henry Clay, had come out against the annexation of the then-independent Republic of Texas as part of the United States. Polk wanted to make Texas a state. Although there were other issues in the presidential campaign, the election of 1844 clearly demonstrated American interest in westward expansion.

Manifest Destiny

In 1845, journalist John L. O'Sullivan captured the nation's feelings when he wrote about "our manifest destiny to overspread and to possess the whole of the continent which Providence has given us for the development of the great experiment of liberty and federated self-government entrusted to us."[6] In the years that followed, expansionist Democrats, in particular, also used the phrase "manifest destiny." They wanted the United States to acquire and settle not just Texas, but also Oregon and California.

Soon enough they would see all their hopes realized. In 1845, Texas entered the Union. In the spring of 1846, Great Britain relinquished its claim to the Oregon Country south of the forty-ninth parallel.

At almost precisely the same time, the Mexican War broke out after Mexican troops attacked American soldiers who had crossed the Nueces River and were headed toward the Rio Grande. President Polk immediately asked Congress for an appropriation of $10 million to fight a war with Mexico. In September 1847, American General Winfield Scott occupied Mexico City. Mexico lost the war. By the Treaty of Guadalupe Hidalgo, signed on February 2, 1848, Mexico ceded to the United States the disputed area of Texas (recognizing the Rio Grande as the its boundary), New Mexico, and California. Out of the land acquired from the Mexican War came the present states of California, Nevada, New Mexico, most of Arizona, and parts of Colorado and Wyoming.

Some especially greedy expansionists continued to call for further American expansion, claiming that the nation should have received all of Mexico under the Treaty of Guadalupe Hidalgo. But most Americans felt satisfied when the United States came to stretch from ocean to ocean.[7] Only in later years would they see that expansion also had its costs.

THE EXISTING STATE OF RELATIONS BETWEEN THE UNITED STATES AND MEXICO RENDERS IT PROPER THAT I SHOULD BRING THE SUBJECT TO THE CONSIDERATION OF CONGRESS. . . .

AS WAR EXISTS, AND NOTWITHSTANDING ALL OUR EFFORTS TO AVOID IT, EXISTS BY THE ACT OF MEXICO HERSELF, WE ARE CALLED UPON BY EVERY CONSIDERATION OF DUTY AND PATRIOTISM TO VINDICATE WITH DECISION THE HONOR, RIGHTS, AND THE INTERESTS OF OUR COUNTRY. . . .

IN FURTHER VINDICATION OF OUR RIGHTS AND DEFENSE OF OUR TERRITORY, I INVOKE THE PROMPT ACTION OF CONGRESS TO RECOGNIZE THE EXISTENCE OF THE WAR, AND TO PLACE AT THE DISPOSITION OF THE EXECUTIVE THE MEANS OF PROSECUTING THE WAR WITH VIGOR, AND THUS HASTENING THE RESTORATION OF PEACE. . . .[8]

President James Polk delivered this speech, asking Congress to declare war on Mexico. The Mexican War helped win additional territory for the United States.

Further Settlement

Many Americans began to move to the West in the 1840s. First, families began to make their way along the Oregon Trail to the Willamette Valley near the mouth of the Columbia River on the Pacific Ocean. (Today, the Columbia, which rises in Canadian British Columbia, serves as the border between the states of Washington and Oregon.) The first wagon train completed the journey in 1842. By 1850, the white population of Oregon had swelled to over thirteen thousand. Ten years later, it had reached fifty-two thousand.[9]

Soon after emigrants began to travel the Oregon Trail, members of the Church of Jesus Christ of Latter-day Saints (often referred to as Mormons) left Illinois to build a new settlement near the Great Salt Lake in Utah. Thanks to their efforts at migration, in 1860, Utah also recorded more than forty thousand residents.

But by far the biggest wave of emigration followed the news that gold had been discovered in California. The Forty-Niners—among whom were people not just from the United States but Europe, Australia, China, and South America—flocked to California in even greater numbers.[10]

Those who traveled overland to Utah, Oregon, and California all crossed the Louisiana Purchase, but generally did not settle there. That region of the country would only become heavily populated later. At the time, it failed to hold the appeal that the Pacific Coast did because gold had not been discovered there. Of

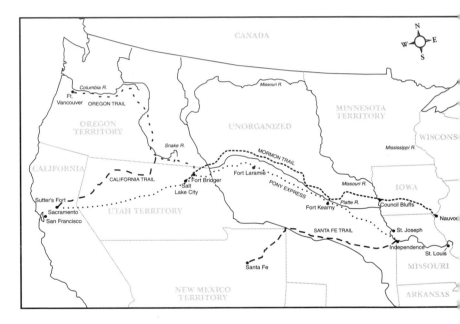

In the 1840s, Americans began to settle the territory of the Louisiana Purchase and the lands beyond. Several trails were established to help settlers travel to the West.

course, the Louisiana Territory had never received the publicity the Oregon Country enjoyed. Americans also thought of the vast Louisiana Territory as empty, lonely, and harsh. It would take the building of the transcontinental railroad to persuade many Americans to move to the West.

7

THE LOUISIANA PURCHASE IS SETTLED

California and Oregon quickly became settled by Americans attracted to the territories' many resources. The explorations of the Louisiana Purchase before 1849 had been conducted largely to establish its boundaries or find the easiest way through it. The emigrants who followed these expeditions quite joyfully passed through the Louisiana Purchase on their way to California and Oregon. The "Great American Desert" of Pike and Long was settled much more slowly.

A Transcontinental Railroad Is Proposed

In 1853, Secretary of War Jefferson Davis, responding to popular demand, ordered the Topographical Corps of the United States Army to conduct a series of expeditions across the Louisiana Purchase to find the best route for a transcontinental railroad. Seemingly, the entire nation was interested in seeing train tracks laid from the East Coast to the West. A transcontinental railroad would be used heavily to ship goods and carry

Secretary of War Jefferson Davis ordered a series of expeditions to find a route across the Louisiana Purchase to build a transcontinental railroad.

passengers. Before such a railroad could be built, Congress needed to decide on a feasible route—one that would be relatively cheap and easy to follow.

Many speculators and investors in railroad companies had a vested interest in which route would be chosen. A great deal of money could be made by those who owned the land through which the transcontinental railroad would run. Settlements at railroad stops—where people boarded and got off—could also be expected to prosper enormously. Because of this potential for profit, rivalries developed among cities. Promoters pointed out the virtues of New Orleans, St. Louis, Chicago, Duluth, Springfield, and other cities to congressmen and at railroad conventions.

Three main expeditions sought the best transcontinental railroad route. (As part of the fourth, lesser, southern expedition, army Lieutenant John G. Parke explored from San Diego to the Rio Grande, and Lieutenant John Pope led a party from the Rio Grande to the Red River. This expedition never entered the Louisiana Purchase.)

The Northern Route

Isaac Stevens, governor of the territory of Washington, commanded the search for a northern route from the Great Lakes across the present-day states of Minnesota, North Dakota, Montana, and Washington to the Pacific Coast. Stevens had already surveyed the land between Lake Superior and St. Paul, Minnesota, looking for feasible routes. On June 6, 1853, he led a group that included army officers, two civilian engineers, an artist, a geologist, and a naturalist from St. Paul up through the Minnesota Territory and north of the Great Bend of the Missouri River to Fort Union, located at the junction of the Missouri and Yellowstone rivers.[1]

From there, the men under Stevens's command took many side trips, exploring as far south as the Black Hills and as far north as the Canadian Border. They were looking for passes in the Rocky Mountains, where the Missouri and the Columbia river systems separate. The entire Stevens party reunited at Fort Benton in Montana, then headed over the Continental Divide and through the Bitterroot Mountains. They located five passes across the Rocky Mountains: the Marias, the Lolo, the Hell-Gate, the Lewis and Clark, and Cadotte's Pass.[2] While Stevens and his party headed west, his assistant, Captain George B. McClellan, was in charge of a party that explored the Cascade Mountains of Washington, searching for passes a railroad could use.

Finally, Stevens's men reunited with McClellan's in the Bitterroot Valley. Together they headed north by way of Lakes Pend d'Oreille and Coeur d'Alene. From Fort Colvile, Stevens wanted his party to go through the Snoqualmoo and Nachess passes, but McClellan and another man refused, protesting that their horses were just too tired. They forced the party to detour far south to Fort Walla Walla on the Snake River in southern Washington. They first followed the

Columbia to Fort Vancouver and then north to the Puget Sound. Two members of the Stevens party made especially daring forays. Lieutenant John Mullan explored the Yellowstone River area, home of the Blackfeet Indians, looking for a connection with the Oregon Trail. Naturalist George Suckley traveled by canoe more than one thousand miles from the Bitterroot Valley to the Pacific Ocean.[3]

At the end of the expedition, Stevens submitted a report to Congress, heartily recommending the northern route he had just taken. Suckley, the expedition's naturalist, privately expressed concerns, however. He wrote to his brother, "A road might be built over the tops of the Himalayeh [*sic*] mountains—but no reasonable man would undertake it. I think the same of the Northern route. . . ."[4] He pointed out that the route would require building tunnels two miles long, a lot of strong and high bridges, and that on it, trains would have to take many short and sharp curves.

Gunnison's Survey

The second expedition, looking for a central route between the 38th and 39th parallels, was led by army Lieutenant John W. Gunnison. This route had some ardent supporters, including Senator Thomas Hart Benton and the residents of St. Louis, which would be located along this route.

Gunnison's party set out from Fort Leavenworth on the Missouri River, on June 23, 1853.[5] The party crossed Kansas and Colorado, heading west. In southern

Colorado, the group explored the Rockies' Sangre de Cristo Pass and then Cochetopa Pass, through which advocates of the central route hoped it would prove easy to lay track.[6] Between the passes, Gunnison sent a small party south to try to reach Taos, in New Mexico. When they arrived back reporting success, he knew he would find a new road the military could use to reach Taos.[7] Heading north and west, they entered Utah. There, they found a passage through the Wasach and Pavant mountains. They entered the valley of the Sevier River, where tragedy struck. On the morning of October 26, 1853, Ute Indians attacked their camp, killing Lieutenant Gunnison, topographer Richard Kern, botanist Frederick Creuzefeldt, a Mormon guide, and four other members of the party.[8]

Command fell to Lieutenant E. G. Beckwith, who set out once again, leaving Utah in the spring of 1854. Beckwith and his command found a feasible route from Utah through the Sierra Mountains and into California. But railroad promoters were not nearly as interested in Beckwith's opinion as they would have been in Gunnison's appraisal. His favorable report was largely ignored.[9]

Lieutenant Whipple Takes to the Field

Army Lieutenant Amiel Weeks Whipple was in charge of the third transcontinental railroad survey party. His expedition crossed just a little of the Louisiana Purchase, after leaving Fort Smith on the Arkansas River on July 14, 1853. From there, Whipple would cross what is now Oklahoma, the very northern tip of Texas, New Mexico, and Arizona and enter California. His most important investigations took place between the Zuni Indian villages of New Mexico and the Colorado River. Much of his route took him through terrible, dry desert. Nevertheless, Whipple also submitted a very enthusiastic report to the government. He had found easy mountain passes and fertile land. To a large extent, Whipple demonstrated that the "Great American Desert" was myth.

The Pacific Railroad Reports

Despite all the railroad expeditions' expense and efforts, Congress took no immediate action based on the surveys. A route for the transcontinental railroad would not be chosen until 1861. In 1860, pharmacist "Doc" Strong, who lived in Dutch Flats, California, wrote to railroad engineer Theodore Judah, pointing out that the surveys had missed an easy route through California's Sierra Nevada Mountains. Judah immediately set out for Dutch Flats, where Strong took him up into the mountains between the Yuba and Bear rivers. Historian William H. Goetzmann has described Strong's discovery as a "massive monocline, or inclined ramp . . . the ideal route over the first and steepest crest of the Sierras. . . ."[10]

Nevertheless, the Pacific Railroad surveys did have one notable achievement. In their wake, Congress published thirteen volumes of *Pacific Railroad Reports* between 1854 and 1859. In essence, these reports

BE IT ENACTED, THAT . . . "THE UNION PACIFIC RAILROAD COMPANY" . . . IS HEREBY AUTHORIZED AND EMPOWERED TO LAY OUT, CONSTRUCT, FURNISH, MAINTAIN AND ENJOY A CONTINUOUS RAILROAD AND TELEGRAPH . . . UPON THE ROUTE AND TERMS HEREINAFTER PROVIDED. . . .

SEC. 9. THAT THE LEAVENWORTH, PAWNEE AND WESTERN RAILROAD COMPANY OF KANSAS ARE HEREBY AUTHORIZED TO CONSTRUCT A RAILROAD AND TELEGRAPH LINE . . . UPON THE SAME TERMS AND CONDITIONS IN ALL RESPECTS AS ARE PROVIDED [FOR CONSTRUCTION OF THE UNION PACIFIC RAILROAD]. . . . THE CENTRAL PACIFIC RAILROAD COMPANY OF CALIFORNIA ARE HEREBY AUTHORIZED TO CONSTRUCT A RAILROAD AND TELEGRAPH LINE FROM THE PACIFIC COAST . . . TO THE EASTERN BOUNDARIES OF CALIFORNIA, UPON THE SAME TERMS AND CONDITIONS IN ALL RESPECTS [AS ARE PROVIDED FOR THE UNION PACIFIC RAILROAD].

SEC. 11. THAT FOR THREE HUNDRED MILES OF SAID ROAD MOST MOUNTAINOUS AND DIFFICULT OF CONSTRUCTION, TO WIT: ONE HUNDRED AND FIFTY MILES WESTERLY FROM THE EASTERN BASE OF THE ROCKY MOUNTAINS, AND ONE HUNDRED AND FIFTY MILES EASTWARDLY FROM THE WESTERN BASE OF THE SIERRA NEVADA MOUNTAINS . . . THE BONDS TO BE ISSUED TO AID IN THE CONSTRUCTION THEREOF SHALL BE TREBLE THE NUMBER PER MILE HEREINBEFORE PROVIDED . . . ; AND BETWEEN THE SECTIONS LAST NAMED OF ONE HUNDRED AND FIFTY MILES EACH, THE CONSTRUCTION THEREOF SHALL BE DOUBLE THE NUMBER PER MILE FIRST MENTIONED. . . .[11]

The Pacific Railway Act of July 1862 authorized the building of the first American transcontinental railroad.

served as an enormous encyclopedia of the West. They included far more than discussions of topography. The many scientists who had accompanied the exploring expeditions also submitted reports on botany, zoology, Indians, and the potential for agriculture. In addition, the reports contained many breathtaking views of the landscape—sketches, engravings, and photographs— and a series of detailed, accurate maps.

The Great Surveys

The final exploration of the West, including lands that entered the Union under the Louisiana Purchase, occurred in the late 1860s and 1870s, when the army

John Wesley Powell and the members of his expedition started from Green River Station, Wyoming Territory, to begin one of their exploration trips through the Grand Canyon.

The Hayden expedition, some of whose members are seen here, surveyed many of the lands of the Louisiana Purchase and other new territories.

sponsored the Great Surveys. John Wesley Powell led parties on a daring boat ride down the Colorado River through the Grand Canyon and then went on to explore more of Arizona, California, Utah, and Wyoming. A survey by Clarence King along the 40th parallel eventually reached from the Rocky Mountains of Wyoming and Colorado to the Sierra Nevadas of California. George Wheeler explored the southern deserts of the Great Basin. And, finally, Ferdinand Hayden carefully surveyed Kansas and parts of Wyoming, Idaho, Colorado, and New Mexico. His particular interest, like King's, was in mining. He searched for coal and other minerals in the Rockies. Hayden also deserves special recognition as one of the first explorers ever to see the West as a potential destination for tourists. His photographer, William H. Jackson, took spectacular photographs of the Yellowstone geysers in 1871. Painter Thomas Moran also accompanied him and produced romantic paintings of the wonders of the West. In 1871, Hayden promoted a bill in Congress to set Yellowstone aside as a national park. When President Ulysses S. Grant signed the bill into law in 1872, the first national park was formed.[12]

Although it was one of the most notable events in American history, the Louisiana Purchase did adversely affect one large group of people: the American Indians who lived in the territory. Historians estimate that at least two hundred thousand Indians resided in those lands.[1] Although some held out for more than fifty years, all the tribes living in the Purchase eventually had to change their way of life, very much against their will. In some cases, war and disease drastically reduced the population of Purchase tribes. Others lost fewer members to death, but all tribes were eventually moved off the lands that had been theirs for generations, onto reservations.

LEGACY OF THE LOUISIANA PURCHASE

Natural Resources

The Louisiana Purchase brought some of the nation's most important natural resources and remarkable landmarks into the United States. First and foremost, the Purchase secured for Americans all rights to the

Mississippi River, which has the third largest drainage system of all the world's rivers. The Mississippi's many tributaries also became American, including, most important, the Missouri, the continent's longest river. Today, the Mississippi continues to be an important economic resource for many major American cities, including St. Louis, Missouri, and New Orleans, Louisiana. In the nineteenth century, steamboats carried cargo and passengers up the river. Coal, petroleum products, sand, gravel, and grain still make their way down the Mississippi in enormous quantities today.

The Great Plains, which for decades have served as the American breadbasket, also became part of the United States under the Louisiana Purchase. The area remains one of the world's major wheat-growing regions. The Great Plains are also important for mining. In the north, there are enormous coal deposits, and the Great Plains produces more oil than any other place in the United States or Canada.

Spectacular physical features such as the geysers of Yellowstone, the Hot Springs of Arkansas, and the eastern Rockies, including Pike's Peak, are also part of the United States—thanks to that bargain Livingston and Monroe struck on behalf of the American government in 1803.

States of the Louisiana Purchase

The Louisiana Purchase brought into the United States the lands that became the states of Louisiana, Arkansas, Oklahoma, Missouri, North Dakota, Kansas,

Minnesota, South Dakota, Iowa, Nebraska, Colorado, Wyoming, and Montana.

Louisiana was the first of the states carved out of the vast territory of the Louisiana Purchase. It entered the Union in 1812. Once the home of great ancient American Indian Mound Builders, Louisiana boasts the largest Indian earthworks still remaining on the continent. The area that became the state of Louisiana had the largest population in the Purchase when it was made. In the years immediately following the Purchase, settlers trickled in. In the War of 1812, Louisiana was the site of the important Battle of New Orleans, where General Andrew Jackson's defeat of the British secured an American victory. After the Americans won that war, settlers streamed in.

Missouri's first permanent settlement, Saint Genevieve, was built by French settlers around 1750. By the time Congress had approved the Louisiana Purchase, St. Louis was already a flourishing community. By 1817, citizens of the Missouri Territory were lobbying for statehood, but Congress delayed granting it due to the problem of slavery in the territory. The Missouri Compromise of 1820, which allowed Missouri to become a slave state and created a future boundary for free versus slave settlement, solved that. Missouri entered the Union in 1821. From 1820 until the Civil War, Missouri saw spectacular growth. This was due, in large part, to St. Louis's role as the Gateway to the West—the starting point for emigrants headed overland to California or Oregon. Many people moved to St. Louis to provide goods and services to these emigrants. Steamboat traffic on the Mississippi also contributed to the growth of St. Louis and Missouri, as did the arrival of a railroad in 1851.

Europeans first settled what would become the state of Arkansas in 1686, when La Salle's lieutenant, Henri de Tonty, built a trading post at the juncture of the Arkansas and Mississippi rivers. By 1800, four hundred settlers of European descent lived in the area. Congress formed the Arkansas District in 1806 and granted it statehood in 1836.

American Indians controlled what would become the state of Iowa until the 1830s. After the Sac and Mesquaki finally ceded their lands, however, the territory was settled quickly by white Americans. Iowa entered the Union in 1846.

The United States gained lands in the present-day state of Minnesota east of the Mississippi at the end of the Revolutionary War in 1783. Those lands had belonged to the British since the French and Indian War ended in 1763. The lands west of the Mississippi that are now part of the state became American territory under the Louisiana Purchase. In 1820, the army began construction of a fort at the junction of the Minnesota and Mississippi rivers. Minnesota saw only slow settlement, however, until after 1853. Then settlers rushed in, and Minnesota gained statehood in 1858.

Spanish explorer Francisco Vásquez de Coronado was the first European to enter the territory that would later become the state of Kansas. For decades after these lands were acquired by the United States as part of the Purchase, they remained unsettled. In the 1830s and 1840s, the federal government relocated American Indians from east of the Mississippi to present-day Kansas. White people were forbidden to settle there, although thousands passed through on their way to Oregon or down the Santa Fe Trail. In the 1850s, gold rushes in Colorado and western Kansas brought miners into the area. The Kansas-Nebraska Act of 1854, which left the question of whether to be a slave state or free state open to settlers, also brought a flood of settlers, who came to make their voices heard on the slavery question. Kansas became a state in 1861.

Explorers Zebulon Pike and Stephen Long were among the first Americans to see the lands that would become Nebraska. Its first permanent settlement was Bellevue, established in 1823. Thousands of emigrants followed Nebraska's Platte River on their way along the Oregon Trail. By 1854, American Indians had ceded most of their lands in eastern Nebraska to the United States, which increased white settlement. The Homestead Act of 1862 further encouraged settlement, as did the building of the transcontinental railroad through the territory. Nebraska became a state in 1867.

Colorado straddles the Continental Divide, so the eastern section of the state was part of the Louisiana Purchase. In 1848, Mexico ceded southern and western Colorado to the United States after its defeat in the

The transcontinental railroad was finally completed on May 10, 1869, with the ceremony seen here. It became an important factor in the settlement of the West.

Mexican War. Prospectors flocked into the state after gold was discovered in Denver in 1858. By 1867, the army had forced all the American Indians except for the Ute out of the state and into Indian Territory, which would later become Oklahoma. Colorado became a state during the nation's centennial in 1876.

French explorers had ventured into the territory that would become North Dakota in 1738. Fifty years later, fur traders returned, and trading posts operated there into the 1830s. In 1812, Scottish and Irish immigrants arrived to establish a community in what would become North Dakota. Ongoing conflicts with American Indians severely curtailed settlement for years. The discovery of gold in the Black Hills, however, brought miners into the area. Agriculture developed rapidly in eastern North Dakota in the 1870s and 1880s, and in western North Dakota in the 1880s and 1890s. South Dakota east of the Mississippi also became settled by the mid-1880s. North Dakota and South Dakota both entered the Union in November 1889.

Montana also became a state in 1889. Fur traders entered this area very early, following the route taken by Lewis and Clark. A gold rush in 1862 brought in a wave of miners. Cattle ranching also became important in Montana in the 1860s. Conflicts with Indians continued to keep many settlers out of Montana, however, for more than twenty more years. In 1880, the population of Montana was 39,159. By 1900, it had increased to over 240,000.[2]

Today, Wyoming remains the least populated of all the American states. Between 1841 and 1868, about 350,000 emigrants passed through Wyoming on their way to Oregon and California. The hostile Teton Sioux, however, prevented permanent settlement there until all the Indians who had resided in Wyoming were on reservations, which occurred by 1877. Congress carved the Wyoming Territory out of the Dakota, Utah, and Idaho territories in 1868. Wyoming did not become a state, however, until 1890.

The federal government removed American Indians from east of the Mississippi to what would later become Oklahoma beginning soon after the Louisiana Purchase. The Choctaw, Chicasaw, Creek, Seminole, and Cherokee tribes were forced to move there after the War of 1812. Congress formally created the Indian Territory in 1834, which then included much of Kansas and Nebraska as well as all of Oklahoma.

In 1838–1839, large numbers of Cherokee and other tribes were forcibly removed to the Indian Territory on a devastating march that has come to be called the Trail of Tears. Kansas and Nebraska had been removed from the Indian Territory by the 1860s, but many reservations continued to be established in what remained. Although federal law prohibited white settlement in the Indian Territory, white ranchers started to lease land from American Indians there in the 1870s. In 1889, the government opened an area in the center of the Indian Territory to white settlement. One

The Louisiana Purchase was carved to produce many of the modern states that belong to the United States, seen here with the dates they entered the Union.

year later, this area was formally declared the Oklahoma Territory. In 1907, the Oklahoma Territory and the Indian Territory united to enter the Union as the state of Oklahoma.

The Louisiana Purchase–Alaska Connection

In some ways, President Thomas Jefferson seized an extraordinary amount of power when he authorized the purchase of Louisiana. According to the Constitution, treaties are really supposed to be a matter for Congress, not the president and the executive branch of the government. In fact, in the early years of the American republic, it was not even entirely clear whether the United States could legally buy new territory under the Constitution. In making the purchase without congressional approval, Jefferson set a precedent for other presidents to follow. For example, in 1867, President Andrew Johnson allowed Secretary of State William H. Seward to negotiate a treaty with Russia, which added the territory of Alaska to the United States.

Legacy

In 1803, headlines trumpeted news of the Louisiana Purchase. Newspapers ran the entire text of the purchase agreements on their front pages. Today, historians still rank the Purchase among the most significant events in American history.

In 1904, St. Louis, Missouri, celebrated the centennial of the Louisiana Purchase by hosting a World's

Fair. Thousands of people visited the fairgrounds, where they strolled through pavilions showcasing American achievements. The anniversaries of the Purchase are still celebrated with museum exhibits and other events today.

The Louisiana Purchase nearly doubled the size of the young American nation. Surveys eventually showed that the Mississippi River drains a million square miles to its west.[3] After its boundaries had finally been settled, the Purchase contained about 828,000 square miles.[4] Today, the lands acquired under the Purchase still make up a huge portion of the continental United States.

Millions of Americans now live in the territory bought by President Thomas Jefferson in 1803. Many others visit every year. Vacation attractions such as Yellowstone National Park, Glacier National Park, Mount Rushmore, and ski resorts such as Vail, Colorado, lie within the Louisiana Purchase. The West has always sparked Americans' imagination. Today, it continues to represent to many people a rich land of opportunity and excitement.

★ TIMELINE ★

1541—*May 8*: Hernando de Soto and his army come upon the Mississippi River about thirty miles south of Memphis, Tennessee.

1682—*April 9*: René-Robert Cavelier, Sieur de La Salle, holds ceremony and claims the entire Mississippi River basin for his king.

1699—*February*: Pierre Le Moyne, Sieur d'Iberville, establishes the first French colony of Louisiana.

1718—Jean-Baptiste Le Moyne, Sieur de Bienville, founds New Orleans.

1764—Auguste Chouteau founds St. Louis.

1793—Alexander Mackenzie, acting on behalf of the British and the North West Company that traded in furs, becomes the first man known to have crossed the North American continent, traveling across all of Canada to the Pacific Ocean.

1803—*April 30*: Robert Livingston and James Monroe make the Louisiana Purchase with France.

1804—*May 14*: Lewis and Clark expedition sets off, destined to become the first group of Americans to cross the continent.

1805—*August*: Lieutenant Zebulon Pike sets out on an exploring expedition, searching for headwaters of the Mississippi River.

1806—*July*: Pike sets off on another expedition, this one supposedly to the headwaters of the Red River.

1806—*September*: Lewis and Clark arrive back in St. Louis.

1810—*Autumn*: John Jacob Astor sends American fur traders to the Pacific Northwest.

1812—Louisiana becomes a state.

1818—*October*: Great Britain and the United States reach an agreement concerning the northern boundary of the United States; They also agree to jointly occupy Oregon.

1819—*February*: The Adams-Onis Treaty finally settles the Louisiana Purchase boundaries.

1820—Stephen Long explores the Great Plains.

1821—Missouri becomes a state.

1825—*July*: Mountain men rendezvous for the first time; It will become a tradition held until the 1840s.

1836—Arkansas becomes a state.

1841—*Spring*: The first emigrant train sets off for Oregon.

1846—Iowa becomes a state.

1848—*January*: The California Gold Rush begins.

1858—Minnesota becomes a state.

1861—Kansas becomes a state.

1867—Nebraska becomes a state.

1876—Colorado becomes a state.

1889—North Dakota, South Dakota, and Montana become states.

1890—Wyoming becomes a state.

1907—Oklahoma becomes a state.

★ CHAPTER NOTES ★

Chapter 1. The "Greatest Real Estate Deal in History"

1. National Archives and Records Administration, "Exhibit: The Louisiana Purchase," *National Archives and Records Administration Home Page*, March 1996, <http://www.nara.gov/exhall/originals/loupurch.html>, (July 9, 1999).

2. *Alistair Cooke's America* (New York: Alfred A. Knopf, 1973), p. 162.

3. Marshall Sprague, *So Vast So Beautiful a Land: Louisiana and the Purchase* (Boston: Little, Brown and Company, 1974), p. xvii.

4. Ibid., pp. 181–183.

5. The Avalon Project, "Treaty of San Ildefonso: October 1, 1800," *The Avalon Project at the Yale Law School: Documents in Law, History, and Diplomacy*, 1997, <http://www.yale.edu/lawweb/avalon/ildefens.html>, (July 9, 1999).

6. Louisiana State Museum, "Louisiana History at the Cabildo, Louisiana History Lesson Plan 3: The Louisiana Purchase," *Louisiana State Museum,* n.d., <http://www.crt.state.la.us/crt/museum/education/lesson3.htm>, (July 9, 1999).

7. Ibid.

8. Donald Jackson, *Thomas Jefferson and the Stony Mountains* (Urbana: University of Illinois Press, 1981), pp. 60–61.

9. Sprague, p. 261.

10. Ibid., p. 287.

11. Ibid., p. 295.

12. Ibid., p. 300.

13. Ibid., p. 302.

14. Ibid., p. 303.

15. Ibid., p. 304.

16. Ibid., p. 311.

17. Quoted in Jerome Agel, *Words That Make America Great* (New York: Random House, 1997), p. 81.

18. Quoted in Sprague, pp. 314, 315.

19. National Archives and Records Administration, "Exhibit: The Louisiana Purchase," *Louisiana Purchase,* March 1996, <http://www.nara.gov/exhall/originals/loupurch.html>.

Chapter 2. Louisiana Under Foreign Flags

1. W. J. Eccles, *France in America* (New York: Harper & Row, 1972), p. 1.

2. Ibid.

3. Paul S. Boyer et al., *The Enduring Vision: A History of the American People* (Lexington, Mass.: D. C. Heath, 1993), p. 36.

4. William H. Goetzmann and Glyndwr Williams, *The Atlas of North American Exploration* (New York: Prentice Hall, 1992), pp. 24–25.

5. Eccles, p. 2.

6. Ibid., pp. 3–5.

7. Goetzmann and Williams, p. 26.

8. Boyer, p. 42.

9. Ibid., p. 42.

10. Ibid., pp. 46–47.

11. Ibid., p. 47.

12. Goetzmann and Williams, pp. 34–35.

13. David Ewing Duncan, *Hernando de Soto: A Savage Quest in the Americas* (New York: Crown, 1995), pp. 401–402.

14. Ibid., pp. 418, 424.

15. Ibid., pp. 424–425.

16. Marshall Sprague, *So Vast So Beautiful a Land: Louisiana and the Purchase* (Boston: Little, Brown and Company, 1974), p. 9.

17. Ibid., p. 12.

18. Goetzmann and Williams, p. 62.

19. Ibid., pp. 62–63.

20. Francis Parkman, *La Salle and the Discovery of the Great West* (Williamstown, Mass.: Corner House Publishers, 1897, reprinted 1968), p. 10.

21. Goetzmann and Williams, p. 65.

22. Sprague, p. 3.

23. Parkman, p. 306.

24. Sprague, p. 4.

25. Ibid., p. 71.

26. Ibid., p. 75.

27. Ibid., p. 85.

28. Louisiana State Museum, "Louisiana History at the Cabildo, Louisiana History Lesson Plan 2: Colonial Louisiana," *Louisiana State Museum,* n.d., http://www.crt.state.la.us/crt/museum/education/lesson2.htm >, (July 9, 1999).

29. Sprague, pp. 108–109.

30. Ibid., p. 109.

31. Ibid., p. 128.

32. Ibid., p. 122.

33. Ibid., p. 154.

34. Ibid., p. 185.

35. Ibid., p. 186.

36. Ibid., p. 187.

Chapter 3. Lewis and Clark

1. Donald Jackson, *Thomas Jefferson and the Stony Mountains* (Urbana: University of Illinois, 1981), pp. 130–131.

2. Ibid., pp. 6–7.

3. Ibid., p. 8.

4. Ibid., p. 104.

5. Ibid., p. xi.

6. Ibid., p. ix.

7. Ibid., p. 57.

8. Ibid., p. 295.

9. Ibid.

10. Ibid., pp. 42–43.

11. Ibid., p. 48.

12. Ibid., p. 61.

13. William H. Goetzmann, *New Lands, New Men* (New York: Viking Penguin, 1986), p. 110.

14. Jackson, p. 76.

15. Ibid., p. 78.

16. Ibid., p. 125.

17. William H. Goetzmann, *Exploring the American West, 1803–1879* (United States National Park Service, Division of Publications, 1982), p. 21.

18. Jackson, p. 136.

19. Quoted in Sanford Wexler, *Westward Expansion: An Eyewitness History* (New York: Facts on File, 1991), pp. 52–53.

20. Jackson, p. 141.

21. Ibid., p. 153.

22. Goetzmann, *Exploring the American West*, p. 24.

23. Ibid., p. 26.

24. Goetzmann, *New Lands, New Men*, p. 102.

25. Jackson, p. 111.

26. Ibid., p. 99.

27. Ibid., p. 103.

28. Ibid., p. 34.

29. Ibid., p. 203.

Chapter 4. The Mountain Men

1. William H. Goetzmann, *Exploring the American West, 1803–1879* (United States National Park Service, Division of Publications, 1982), p. 41.

2. William H. Goetzmann and Glyndwr Williams, *The Atlas of North American Exploration* (New York: Prentice Hall, 1992), pp. 142–143; Goetzmann, *Exploring the American West*, pp. 32–33.

3. William H. Goetzmann, *Exploration and Empire* (New York: Knopf, 1966), p. 33.

4. Goetzmann and Williams, *The Atlas of North American Exploration*, p. 143.

5. Donald Jackson, *Thomas Jefferson and the Stony Mountains* (Urbana: University of Illinois, 1981), p. 285.

6. Goetzmann, *Exploring the American West*, p. 45.

7. Goetzmann and Williams, *The Atlas of North American Exploration*, p. 151; Goetzmann, *Exploration and Empire*, p. 111.

8. Goetzmann and Williams, *The Atlas of North American Exploration*, p. 151.

9. Dale L. Morgan, *Jedediah Smith and the Opening of the West* (New York: Bobbs-Merrill Co., 1953), p. 23.

10. LeRoy R. Hafen, ed., *Mountain Men and Fur Traders of the Far West* (Lincoln: University of Nebraska Press, 1982), p. 93; Morgan, p. 30.

11. William Goetzmann, *Exploration and Empire*, pp. 114–115; Morgan, pp. 84–85.

12. Goetzmann, *Exploring the American West*, p. 46.

Chapter 5. Establishing the Boundaries

1. National Archives and Records Administration, "Exhibit: The Louisiana Purchase," *National Archives and Records Administration Home Page*, March 1996, <http://www.nara.gov/exhall/originals/louistxt.html>, (July 9, 1999.).

2. Donald Jackson, *Thomas Jefferson and the Stony Mountains* (Urbana: University of Illinois Press, 1981), p. 108.

3. Ibid.

4. Ibid., p. 231.

5. Ibid., p. 244.

6. Ibid., pp. 244–245.

7. William H. Goetzmann, *Exploration and Empire* (New York: Knopf, 1966), p. 44.

8. Ibid.

9. Jackson, p. 247.

10. Goetzmann, p. 47.

11. Jackson, p. 252.

12. Goetzmann, p. 49.

13. Ibid., p. 51.

14. Ibid.

15. Helen Hornbeck Tanner, ed., *The Settling of North America: The Atlas of the Great Migrations into North America from the Ice Age to the Present* (New York: Macmillan, 1995), p. 81.

16. William H. Goetzmann and Glyndwr Williams, *The Atlas of North American Exploration* (New York: Prentice Hall, 1992), p. 144.

17. William H. Goetzmann, *Exploring the American West, 1803-1879* (United States National Park Service, Division of Publications, 1982), pp. 32–33.

18. Tanner, p. 81.

19. Quoted in Jerome B. Agel, *Words That Make America Great* (New York: Random House, 1997), pp. 86–87.

20. Goetzmann and Williams, *The Atlas of North American Exploration*, pp. 156–157.

Chapter 6. The Idea of Expansion

1. *Alistair Cooke's America* (New York: Alfred A. Knopf, 1973), p. 156.

2. Paul S. Boyer et al., *The Enduring Vision: A History of the American People* (Lexington, Mass.: D. C. Heath, 1993), p. 107.

3. *Alistair Cooke's America*, p. 158.

4. Boyer, p. 208.

5. Donald Jackson, *Thomas Jefferson and the Stony Mountains* (Urbana: University of Illinois, 1981), p. 298.

6. Boyer, p. 431.

7. Ibid., p. 439.

8. Quoted in Henry Steele Commager, ed., *Documents of American History* (New York: Appleton-Century-Crofts, Inc., 1958), vol. 1, pp. 310–311.

9. Helen Hornbeck Tanner, ed., *The Settling of North America: The Atlas of the Great Migrations into North America from the Ice Age to the Present* (New York: Macmillan, 1995), p. 98.

10. Ibid.

Chapter 7. The Louisiana Purchase Is Settled

1. William H. Goetzmann, *Army Exploration in the American West, 1803–1863* (New Haven and London: Yale University Press, 1979), p. 280.

2. Ibid.

3. Ibid., p. 281.

4. Ibid., p. 283.

5. Ibid., p. 285.

6. Ibid., p. 283.

7. Ibid., p. 285.

8. Ibid.

9. William H. Goetzmann and Glyndwr Williams, *The Atlas of North American Exploration* (New York: Prentice Hall, 1992), pp. 166–167.

10. William H. Goetzmann, *Exploration and Empire* (New York: Knopf, 1966), p. 295.

11. Quoted in Henry Steele Commager, ed., *Documents of American History* (New York: Appleton-Century-Crofts, Inc., 1958), vol. 1, pp. 411–412.

12. William H. Goetzmann, *Exploring the American West, 1803–1879* (United States National Park Service, Division of Publications, 1982), pp. 83–93.

Chapter 8. Legacy of the Louisiana Purchase

1. Helen Hornbeck Tanner, ed., *The Settling of North America: The Atlas of the Great Migrations into North America from the Ice Age to the Present* (New York: Macmillan, 1995), p. 48.

2. Encarta Concise Free Encyclopedia, "Montana," *Encarta Online Home Page*, n.d., <http://www.encarta.msn.com>, (July 9, 1999).

3. Marshall Sprague, *So Vast So Beautiful a Land: Louisiana and the Purchase* (Boston: Little, Brown and Company, 1974), p. xvii.

4. Ibid.

★ FURTHER READING ★

Books

Ambrose, Stephen. *Undaunted Courage: Meriwether Lewis, Thomas Jefferson and the Opening of the American West.* New York: Simon & Schuster, 1996.

Edwards, Judith. *Lewis and Clark's Journey of Discovery in American History.* Springfield, N.J.: Enslow Publishers, Inc., 1999.

Goetzmann, William H., and Glyndwr Williams. *The Atlas of North American Exploration.* New York: Prentice Hall, 1992.

Jackson, Donald. *Thomas Jefferson and the Stony Mountains.* Urbana: University of Illinois, 1981.

Tanner, Helen Hornbeck, ed. *The Settling of North America: The Atlas of the Great Migrations into North America from the Ice Age to the Present.* New York: Macmillan, 1995.

Internet Addresses

Louisiana State Museum. "Louisiana History at the Cabildo, Louisiana History Lesson Plan 3: The Louisiana Purchase." *Louisiana State Museum.* n.d. <http://www.crt.state.la.us/crt/museum/education/lesson3.htm> (May 4, 1999).

National Archives and Records Administration. "Exhibit: The Louisiana Purchase." *National Archives and Records Administration Home Page.* March 1996. <http://www.nara.gov/exhall/originals/loupurch.html> (May 4, 1999).

★ INDEX ★